Colette de Bruin

The Essential 5

Written by:
Colette de Bruin

Edited and translated by:
Caroline Hamerslag

Published by:
Graviant educatieve uitgaven,
Doetinchem, The Netherlands

Illustrations and layout:
Wim Harzing

The author's website:
www.geefmede5.com

This book has been translated from Dutch.
Original title: *Geef me de 5*.

© January 2012.

ISBN 978-9491337017

Foreword

I did not quite know what to expect when I made an appointment with Colette to discuss her book 'The Essential 5' which was in the last stages of development. The appointment was made in a minute and soon after we made each other's acquaintance, Colette takes control spontaneously. Lovingly, she talks about her five (foster) children who all have a form of autism and her father who has Asperger disorder. She also talks about her job as a SEN coordinator and she is talking so quickly and keenly that it takes a lot of effort to focus my attention. I really want to do so, because I feel that what she is saying makes a lot of sense. I seem to fail at listening and writing it down at the same time. 'Give it to me,' is Colette's cheerful reaction. Coloured marker pens appear. It only takes her a few minutes to explain how, after observation, I can analyse the problem and which steps must be taken after that. Also: how it can be put into writing concisely. Now that I don't have to write, I pose one question after another. Colette elaborates on her method, video recordings, made-to-measure help and how it should be clear and predictable for the child. This involves five words and when these are used, everything will be alright. I recognize a lot in the images she describes. Thinking: the umpteenth so-called efficient method. How often have I been promised the moon? Then my cell-phone rings. It is my autistic son, meaning a nice woolly conversation is about to follow. He asks where I am and what time I will be home. I tell him that I am at the other side of the country and that I don't know exactly how long it will take and how much time the trip back home takes. Also, I give him some vague instructions. He lingers on the phone and keeps chatting and I chat away, too. When I hang up, Colette starts analysing the situation with unerring instinct and, on the basis of this real life case, starts explaining what it is that this child aims at with this phone-call. I didn't answer his questions, my son does not know where he stands and is left in the dark. I must admit that this is right. I just know he will call back later because it is all unclear to him. Usually these moments are used to chat away merrily with my son, not to exchange actual information. Colette explains to me that for him it is all about that particular information. So when he calls back after a few minutes, I decide to apply the method that was just explained to me. He hangs up after just one minute leaving me in amazement. What is happening here? Again, a laughing Colette gives her vision: 'You see it works!?' Full of enthusiasm I say goodbye, heading home with a sheet full of colours which leave me clueless. The days that follow are full of amazing events. My son asks questions and my replies are such

interview with Agnes Weber, employee Dutch Society for Autism

3

that for him no questions remain open. When I want him to do something, I also use What, How, Where, When and Who as a basis for my answers. Our encounters are brief and our conversations even briefer. He turns around immediately when he gets the information he needs. By making my questions clear he answers of his own accord, but still needing help from time to time. I can see that he performs what I ask of him and also picks up chores self-reliantly, chores which in the past needed a couple of days to 'warm up'. He is very proud which boosts his self-confidence. He is totally ignorant of the fact that there is a book with a method called 'The Essential 5' which I am putting into practice, even before it is published. This method is so simple and so made-to-measure at the same time that it will certain achieve positive results with every person with autism. I am wholly convinced of that.

Thank you, Colette!

Agnes Weber
September 2004

Employee Dutch Society for Autism

Table of contents

Introduction

8

Introduction

While travelling abroad, a long time ago, I was driving along a road lined with shops. I did not know the language of the country I was travelling in. Yet my eyes kept trying to read the words in the shop-windows and on the bill boards – over and over again. Time and again my brain, too, tried in vain to understand those words. I got tired with reading but could not stop except when I closed my eyes. But trying not to be unsociable towards my husband I kept looking. Until suddenly, in a flash, I saw a word: 'banka'. Recognising the familiar word 'bank', I felt much more at peace.

lost…

We drove on and came to a round-about. In the middle was something which looked like a signpost with signs pointing in four different directions. But I could not read what was on them. So we drove around, and around, and around… I really did not know which would be the right road to our final destination. A road map did not help: the tiny villages mentioned were not on it. Asking someone for help? I did not know how. I did not speak their language nor did they speak any English or German.

Many years later this particular moment came back to me when I was talking to people with autism, who in everyday life are just as lost as I was back then, in that country faraway. Imagine that: over and over again, every day, many times a day.

Why this book?
When I started to work with children with autism, I could not find a book which stated in clear terms how to raise these children. Not to mention how to give support to parents during education. Of course, there is plenty of reading material but because of the complexity of the autistic disorder I simply could not find 'handles' for the education of children with autism.

raising a child with autism

Without my knowing it, I had already had quite some experience with autism. I raised children who were later diagnosed with PDD-NOS and it turned out my father had Asperger disorder. I then started to gain more in-depth knowledge on the subject of autism. I was deeply interested in autism and it became more and more familiar to me. I wished to understand how the mind of a child of autism works. While gaining ever more experience, I learned to predict, so to speak, the child's behaviour, which is a result of straightforward thinking. If lots of different children with the same disorder think along similar lines, it makes sense that there is also a univocal manner of dealing with these children. Some kind of education every child with autism benefits from, preferably in a most practical and simple form.

My quest resulted in one clear and simple rule:

Be predictable and clear about

What, How, When, Where and Who

In this book I would like to explain why children with autism need to be raised differently. What this upbringing looks like, why this particular approach really works and how the upbringing can be put into effect in a concrete and practical manner will be demonstrated by real-life examples in this book.

Target group
This book was especially written with a view to the upbringing of children who have PDD- NOS and Asperger disorder. But it also works very well for people with other autistic disorders and provides excellent 'handles' for the support of people who are (severely) mentally impaired. First of all, the book is intended for parents because in the course of my work I was confronted with their feelings of incapacity. Quite a few parents asked me to put into words the 'handles' I used while supporting their children. My practical support and approach have thus taken the shape of this book, so that many more people can share this particular approach of a child with autism.

Attendants other than parents - whether they work as professionals or not - may use this book as a practical instrument. Teachers and social workers working with children with autism or a related contact disorder may also benefit from this book. In short: this book is intended for all those who have something to do with autism.

A better relationship
Having a child with an autistic disorder has major consequences. Some parents have already published on that subject. This book is about something else. I hope it will serve to contribute to a better relationship with these special need children, meaning families will have more space for their other children, for the relationship between parents, social environment and last but not least: for everyone individually.

for whom?

Choices made in this book

This book was written for both parents and attendants, which is why the world 'child' is used throughout. If applicable, this word can be substituted by 'adult' with autism. For the same approach can often be applied in the case of adults with the same disorder. For reasons of readability I chose the word 'autism', meaning classical autism (Kanner's autism), Asperger disorder and PDD-NOS, each with its own breakdowns.

Every child with autism is unique. Apart from this, the autistic disorder manifests itself uniquely in each different child.
The child is bothered by his autism to a smaller or larger degree, depending on the child's mental impairment, the degree of autism and the predictability of his environment. This means you may encounter portions of text which are not - or only partially - relevant to your child. Or that your child's disorder manifests itself in a different manner. It is impossible to match the entire contents to each individual child. For each example and every 'handle' offered goes: read it and match it, match it to your child.

match this book to your child

I chose the male form because most children with autism are boys. But of course 'he' and 'his' can be replaced by 'she' or 'her'. Children's names used in the examples are either fictitious or quoted with the permission of (the child and) the parents. Examples often mention education forms, in order to provide a better picture of the child's intellectual abilities. General education stands for the standard curriculum. Children with learning difficulties can either attend special primary education (SPE) or special secondary education (SSE). Both forms are meant for children with (severe) learning difficulties who have special educational needs (SEN).

Because of my work and family this book has naturally become a very practical one, making its framework not primarily scientific or theoretical. For this, plenty of other very suitable books are at hand. For reasons of readability, behavioural characteristics will be restricted to the most prominent ones.

'The Essential 5'
got its name because in the end every appeal for help from all children with autism is: 'give me a clear answer to the five questions forming the jigsaw puzzle (What, How, Where, When and Who) so I can do what is expected of me.'

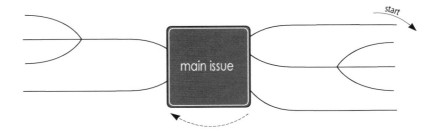

start

Mind map

In my work with children with autism I use a lot of 'mindmapping'. This is a method of organising one's thoughts onto paper. Imagine a mind map as a tree and read it as follows:

-     trunk: main subject;
-     branches: subdivision of main subject;
-     twigs: secondary issues;
-     read clockwise, starting at "ten past one".

'Thank you' to my father who wrote the poems in The Essential 5.

Trust
So often I've bumped my head
So often things went the wrong way
that the word 'trust' is a dead birdie
I am sad to say...

Restoring all that
will take a long time for me
If I hold out long
I'll get rid of the birdie... maybe

Appointments on time
And promises kept
On the basis of mutuality....
How wonderful that will be!

1   What is autism?

Although a lot has been written about autism, it still remains kind of a mystery to many. I will describe in understandable and concrete words what autism really is. Medical and technical terms used have been deliberately incorporated. If desired, these terms can be linked to the entire book which provides accessible reading. The way I describe things makes it easier, in the child's behaviour, to recognise his information processing disorder and the effects thereof on the child's thinking.

1.1 Terms used

Diagnostic reports on children and in literature about autism teem with many different names for autistic disorders. Pervasive Developmental Disorder (PDD), autism spectrum disorders, autism and related social deficit disorders, disorder in the autism spectrum, et cetera. You can hardly see the wood for the trees.

Literature uses collective terms such as PDD (Pervasive Developmental Disorder) and ASD (Autism Spectrum Disorder), which we can see as an umbrella which breaks down into categories as follows :

terms used in literature or diagnostic reports

1 Autistic disorder
2 PDD-NOS (MCDD)
3 Asperger disorder
4 Rett disorder
5 Childhood disintegrative disorder

Again, for reasons of readability, I use the word 'autism'.

Behavioural characteristics

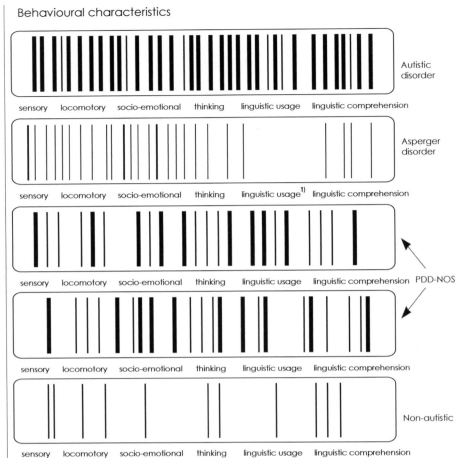

sensory   locomotory   socio-emotional   thinking   linguistic usage   linguistic comprehension — Autistic disorder

sensory   locomotory   socio-emotional   thinking   linguistic usage[1]   linguistic comprehension — Asperger disorder

sensory   locomotory   socio-emotional   thinking   linguistic usage   linguistic comprehension — PDD-NOS

sensory   locomotory   socio-emotional   thinking   linguistic usage   linguistic comprehension

sensory   locomotory   socio-emotional   thinking   linguistic usage   linguistic comprehension — Non-autistic

aren't we all a little autistic?

1) **superficially perfect power of expression** (Gillberg & Gillberg (1998)

Barcode
How can two children both diagnosed with PPD-NOS be so different from each other? Doesn't every individual have a few autistic characteristics? These are questions that I mean to clarify by means of the 'barcode'.

A child with classical autism has many striking behavioural characteristics which make the disorder easily recognisable. If you visualise this in a barcode, then the barcode shows not only a large number of characteristics (lines) but also quite a few bold lines (meaning striking characteristics).

If we visualise the two PDD-NOS children mentioned earlier the result is as follows. One child with PDD-NOS has fewer lines - compared to classical autism - and there's also a smaller amount of bold lines. The other child with PDD-NOS has about the same amount of lines, but thin and bold lines are not in the same place. This is how you can see that both children behave very differently although they share the same disorder.

The last barcode in the picture stands for you and me. Don't we all have some characteristics of autism? I am sure you, too, have certain habits you like to cling to. Or you may hate it when your planning for the day is suddenly disrupted. But it doesn't mean you can be diagnosed with 'autism': for that lines in nearly all development areas are required.

Men are believed to be more autistic in the way they think (analytical thinking) than women. Is that so? Well, at least the last barcode represents the average non-autistic person.

1.2 Consequences
Summarising, the consequences of autism boil down to the following:

The child relating to its environment:
-        falls short of expectations;
-        struggles in relationships to others;
-        a lot of 'miscommunication'.

consequences for the child

Parents:
-        regular upbringing methods do not work;
-        searching for help in an 'assistance jungle';
-        family clashes;
-        relationship between parents under pressure;
-        lack of understanding causes a feeling of being cut-off socially;
-        personal interests must be given up;
-        surviving instead of living.

consequences for the parents

Siblings:
-        must often give up own interests and take the blows;
-        family clashes: mutually as well as with parents;
-        often less attention for siblings of children with autism;
-        have to learn how to live with a challenged/ disabled sibling;
-        reactions from the environment.

consequences for siblings

2 Jigsaw puzzle observation

The perception of people with autism - who suffer from an information processing disorder - differs from ordinary perception: it is fragmented. This different way of observing is the very nucleus of autism, and my starting-point for describing the disorder. If the child perceives in a different manner, it also gives a different meaning to things. We will extensively describe the big consequences this has for the way he thinks. Only if you really understand how a child with autism thinks, you can partially put yourself in his position, which in turn is necessary to properly guide him.

Autism is a congenital brain disorder. We perceive things through eyes, ears, skin, mouth and nose. The information is sent to the brain, compared to previously stored information and processed, and a reaction follows.
For example: outside, you can see someone heading for the front-door, you hear the doorbell, you get up and open the door without even thinking about it. For you there's a logical connection between seeing someone, hearing the bell and opening the door. In a child with autism, opening the door is not necessarily a logical step after hearing the doorbell.

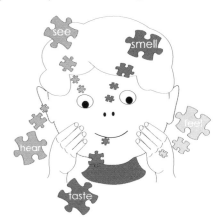

This is caused by what we call 'jigsaw puzzle observation': odd and incomplete bits and pieces of information arrive in the brain, apart from each other: a coherent and meaningful over-all picture is not instantly formed.
The child needs to put the pieces of the puzzle together before he can observe the events as a whole which makes looking for

the right meaning difficult. The brain can do this in a flash, but it still needs to be done.

It's not just the sound of the doorbell: a child with autism must do this puzzling every time he sees, smells, feels, tastes or hears something. You might imagine it takes a lot of hard work - which is done subconsciously, invisibly inside the brain - to process this large amount of information. Things may go wrong, too, when information has been 'mislaid' and therefore cannot be found back. When we look at the example of hearing the bell and opening the door, there is not an obvious connection between the perception of seeing someone
heading for the front-door and hearing the bell on the one hand, and the action (opening the door) on the other. So, it may occur that the child does not open the door, just staying quietly where it is, without even realising that something needs to be done.

When the brain receives a huge amount of information at the same time, all the jigsaw puzzle pieces travel to the brain in which they form a big pile. The child needs to go puzzling first. So for him, processing impressions takes more time. When the child can no longer process the large amount of puzzle pieces you can often see him 'exploding'. Usually this is about something trivial, but it is the proverbial straw that breaks the camel's back (i.e. the last piece of the puzzle that makes him explode).

information must be put together like pieces of a jigsaw puzzle

over-stimulation

Danger of:

Frans van Hout

Luckily the brain works hard to put all the puzzles together. Reaction time may vary from several seconds up to a week or even a month.

Amber, arriving at school, tells her teacher that Sharon is bullying her. The teacher persists and it eventually turns out that this took place at a birthday party several weeks ago.

After the child has put the pieces of the puzzle together, it needs to give a meaning to it. Because of the way he thinks, this, too, is not an easy thing to do.

William tells his teacher angrily: 'Evan wants to hit me.' Evan is put on the spot, but doesn't understand. He merely wanted to do a high-five with William, because they are friends. Then William ran away to go to the teacher. William misinterpreted the meaning of Evan's raised hand.

You can imagine that, the busier the child is, the more information it gets. So it needs to make more jigsaw puzzles and there is a bigger chance of incorrect puzzling.

Emily (11), PPD-NOS, is on a birthday visit at her aunt's, along with her parents and sister. The table has been neatly set and coffee and cake is ready. Emily goes to her sister and doing so, passes the table and brushes aside a cup of coffee which drops. Several people comment on this, but Emily does not have the faintest idea: what does she have to do with the spilt coffee? She blames her sister. Other people think it is odd that an eleven-year-old is blaming someone else who isn't even close to the table, when it is crystal clear that she did it herself. Luckily, Emily's mother knows how her mind works, telling her: 'You didn't know that you knocked over that cup, but your hand did that when you walked past the table. Come make your apologies.' Emily says 'I am sorry' and the other people in the room no longer pay attention to the incident.

Her mother's interference has prevented Emily from being branded. But why does Emily blame her sister? During the incident she was looking at her sister, because that is where she was heading. She puts these two pieces of the puzzle (i.e. the knocking over of the coffee-cup and her sister) together. To her, this is one single image and therefore the right version of the story. Mother helps her by giving her a rule ('Come make your apologies') which makes Emily's conduct socially acceptable.

Chances of incorrect puzzling by an autistic child are plentiful. You hear these children talk and you think: this doesn't match my observations... The child forms an image of an event that doesn't match reality. It has made an incorrect puzzle. Because this incorrect puzzling is done unintentionally, you cannot call tackle the child about his wrong ideas. This is his impairment; the result of his fragmented observation. Therefore do not try to argument about this, because it is his truth.

3 Thinking differently

Because the child observes the world in a different manner, it also thinks differently. In order to raise the child appropriately it is very important to understand the way he thinks.

There are three cognitive theories about thought (with a view to knowledge and language) which clarify most of the conduct demonstrated by autistic children. Knowing these theories can help provide insight into their conduct. I use them as a means to explain the disorder to parents and educators. It also helps to understand behaviour if you know what caused it. In literature, the following terms are used:

- Central coherence. Seeing 'the big picture' and call things by their right names. In other words: observing the surroundings as a whole with everything inside, including persons and communication, and putting the correct meaning on everything. (Baren & Cohen, 1997).
- Executive functions. Planning and organising tasks and demonstrating flexibility in doing so. In other words: What is the order of tasks and How do I perform them (Ozonoff, 1995).
- Theory of mind. Understanding and taking into con sideration the other person's inner self. Moreover, recognising one's own inner self, being able to put it into words and acting according to one's inner self (Frith, 1996).

A child with autism has great difficulties with central coherence (CC) and executive functions (EF) as well as with theory of mind (TOM). The child's different way of thinking has large consequences for his development as a whole. As a result he reacts differently, behaves differently, communicates differently and misinterprets things. How do the consequences of this disorder in CC, EF and TOM affect the child? Here's an illustration followed by an explanation.

thinking differently is especially a characteristic of autism

central coherence

executive functions

theory of mind

19

Fragmented observation and consequences for the mind

Information arrives in jigsaw puzzle pieces

As a result he has...

... trouble seeing 'the big picture' and putting the correct meaning on things
CC = Central Coherence

incorrect puzzling

... difficulties planning and organising
EF = Executive Functions

... difficulties understanding both his own and the other person's behaviour and inner self
TOM = Theory of Mind

3.1 Central coherence (CC)

Because of jigsaw puzzle observation, the child with autism often sees no coherence. He is likely to perceive a situation as a collection of facts, a recital of odd puzzle pieces, failing to see the connection between them and being unable to give the right meaning to things. As a consequence, he may quickly lose track of the situation and panic.

After reading a piece of text, Nadine (12), Higher General Secondary School, can only recount the last phrase, i.e. the most recent puzzle piece. Nor can she answer questions about a text. Still, she is not stupid. She just fails to see the connection between the various phrases. She cannot give meaning to things which cannot literally be found in the text. Therefore she has a limited perception because she is unable to see the 'big picture'.

failing to see the big picture = CC

Sean (10), special school, doesn't want to go to school on Tuesdays anymore. On Monday evenings, he's completely panic-stricken. After persistent questions it turns out that this it is because of the writing-lessons. Because there are so many rules, Sean loses track of the situation all the time. He must process a crammed sheet of paper (i.e. puzzle) over and over again before he can go to work, it drives him 'crazy'. It is agreed with the teacher that Sean is allowed to skip sentences. Blank spaces make the sheet less crammed, which allows him to preserve a clear view. Because he fails to perceive the connection, Sean gets bogged down in details.

Who is up there, is it a bird?
x Who is up there, is it a bird?
x Who is up there, is it a bird?

No, it is Mel with a balloon.
x No, it is Mel with a balloon.
x No, it is Mel with a balloon.

balloons bat bird bus
x balloons bat bird bus
x balloons bat bird bus

Unchanging details are vitally important to autistic children.
The child cannot see the 'big picture', which prevents him from
discerning the difference between essentials and details.
The only thing he can do is hold on details. We also call this
'thinking in details '.
This way of thinking has two outlets, the first of which can be
seen in a child that does not understand something until all
details (puzzle pieces) he keeps in his head, are also fully
present in real life.

*John cannot enjoy his birthday party until all the guests he
expects have arrived and until he has been given all the
presents on his wish-list.*

The second form can be seen in children who start performing a
task immediately upon seeing one single detail, whether this fits
the situation at hand or not.

*Gerry (16), special secondary school, sees gravel and a large
wrought-iron gate near a mansion. His conclusion: this is a
graveyard. (For Gerry the two elements 'gravel' and 'gate' =
graveyard).*

*Benjamin (9), special primary school, and his mother go to a
snack bar to get chips. On one of the tables he sees a glass
which has been left half-full.   Benjamin does not think twice,
picks up the glass and empties it. For him goes: seeing a drink =
drinking it.*

*Syntha (11), special primary school, always counts the number
of eggs their chickens produce. And every day she asks her
mother how many eggs she has used. This is how she keeps
track of the eggs in stock. When her mother gives away a box
of eggs, Syntha immediately notices. Knowing how many eggs
there are, gives her something to hold on to. That is why her
mother prepares her for the fact that later on ten eggs will be
missing.*

When, with the help of 'The Essential 5', her life has been made
clearer and more predictable, she does no longer need the
counting of the eggs to keep her grip.

It can be difficult for a child with autism to perform an action which was previously learned in a similar situation. Situations must be the same, down to the very last detail for him to be able to perform the action.

Stephen (9), special primary school, can unscrew his drink bottle by himself. He empties it and then puts the lid back on the bottle without closing it. This is something he is unable to do, because he fails to understand that closing the bottle is the opposite of unscrewing it.

Daniel (3), special preschool education, cannot go up and down stairs at home. But at his daytime playgroup he goes up and down stairs along with the other children without any trouble.

Caitlin (17), special secondary school, is afraid of a great number of things. Going to school, riding in a taxi. Falling, or her lunch box bursting open. She is afraid to get dirty, or being unable to finish her food, or not liking her food. These often imaginary fears and worries about what will be and may never even take place, take away her pleasure in life. That is because Caitlin herself cannot generalise and put things into perspective. Her surroundings can help her doing so. For example by repeating over and over again: 'All people get dirty, that is part of life' (generalising) or by saying: 'You can wash that off in no-time' (putting things into perspective). Caitlin will link this phrase with getting dirty, which will replace the folder 'Fear' (see Chapter 4).

generalising

For the autistic child, giving a meaning to the observation means extra time to think. For example, when he sees a marker pen: the initial observation is made in jigsaw puzzle pieces. When the puzzle in his head is complete, he needs to give the correct meaning to it. This, too, goes step by step.

- Step 1: His observation. He observes a long, thin, red plastic thing and he sees a short, white, short thing.
- Step 2: He gives meaning to it. He notices that the two items are connected and he recognises the object.

giving meaning

- Step 3: He looks for a word to describe it: it is a 'marker pen'.
- Step 4: Now he knows what he can do with it: drawing on a piece of paper. (Van Dalen, 1994)

This high speed process takes place little by little. But every time the child looks at the paper and then again at the marker pen, he must go through the same four steps over and over again. This also applies to everything he hears, feels, tastes or smells. Compared to a non-autistic person the child therefore must deal with a huge extra amount of mind work (puzzles). Sometimes the child makes a permanent connection between details in one of these steps: giving of meaning. Thus, incorrect and absolute connections are made. This is also referred to as '1-1 association'.

1-1 association

Jasmine (6) drinks orange juice from a green mug. It turns out the orange juice is off. Consequence: Jasmine never wants to drink from a green mug again.

John (17) falls from the stairs, at the exact same moment his father arrives. Unconsciously, he makes a connection between 'Dad' and 'falling from the stairs' and thus blames his father.

Edward's (13) tyre is punctured when he rides his bike through pieces of broken glass. Some years later he rides his bike through broken glass again, gets off his bike and covers the remaining two miles by foot. At home it turns out that the tyre is still intact, but Edward persists: 'I rode through broken glass, so I have a puncture.' The first experience is an established fact. He links, makes the wrong connection and associates: glass = puncture, so I have to walk.

3.2 Executive functions (EF)
Doing something which involves a number of subsequent actions to be performed in the correct order, requires organisation and planning. A child with autism who has difficulty seeing the big picture, therefore also has trouble planning and organising his own tasks.

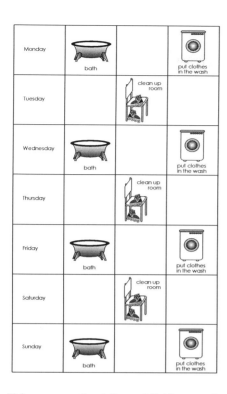

Monday	bath		put clothes in the wash
Tuesday		clean up room	
Wednesday	bath		put clothes in the wash
Thursday		clean up room	
Friday	bath		put clothes in the wash
Saturday		clean up room	
Sunday	bath		put clothes in the wash

difficulty planning and organising tasks = EF

This means that the child has not yet got the hang of activities which, given his age, he should have mastered a long time ago (e.g. brushing his teeth, taking a shower, picking his clothes). If, however, things are planned for him, it means that he can hold on to that and he will be capable of taking action. There will, however, always be an initial resistance against changes he has not come up with himself.

3.3 Theory of mind (TOM)
Young children have difficulty putting themselves in someone else's shoes; they take their own needs as a starting-point. They cannot yet indicate why they have those needs. Generally speaking a child learns that the other person also has an inner self, with its own opinions, plans, intentions and emotions. Being able to see one's own and the other person's inner self as well as taking it into consideration, is called 'theory of mind' (TOM).

difficulty putting
oneself in
someone else's
shoes and
taking into
consideration the
other person's
inner self = TOM

Children with autism have a faulty TOM. It is hard for them to feel that someone else has his own personal inner self. They cannot understand why the other person's perception of reality should be different from their own's. (It is wise not to try to enter into a discussion about this).

The child does not understand the other person's behaviour and emotions which, consequently, are almost impossible for him to predict, too. Apart from this, the perception that the other person may have thoughts about his own inner self, is confined to just a handful of autistic persons, making manipulating virtually impossible. Also, the child has difficulty under-standing and phrasing his own inner self, his motives, emotions and opinions, and observing his own part in a given situation. If, for example, the child kicks someone, it may be quite possible that he does not understand he is hurting someone. Or his judgment may be harsh, without taking into consideration the other person's feelings, like: 'You stink' or 'I hate your clothes'.

I once heard about an autistic man who walked away from his wife's confinement, because he had to attend classes.

Ball games address CC, EF and TOM at the same time. For most children with autism, participating in ball games is not their lot in life (e.g. in a team). The child must be able to plan (EF) steps in order to get the ball into the right place. For this, he needs to be able to see the big picture (CC). Also, he must be able to evaluate his teammates' and opponents' intentions (TOM). Because of his possible sensory sensitivities (see Chapter 5), he prefers not to be touched, so he stays on the edges which is at the expense of the game. What is more: he must be able to remember the rules of the game in case this becomes necessary. One can understand that doing all of this is just too difficult for many autistic children.

Reflected in a diagram:

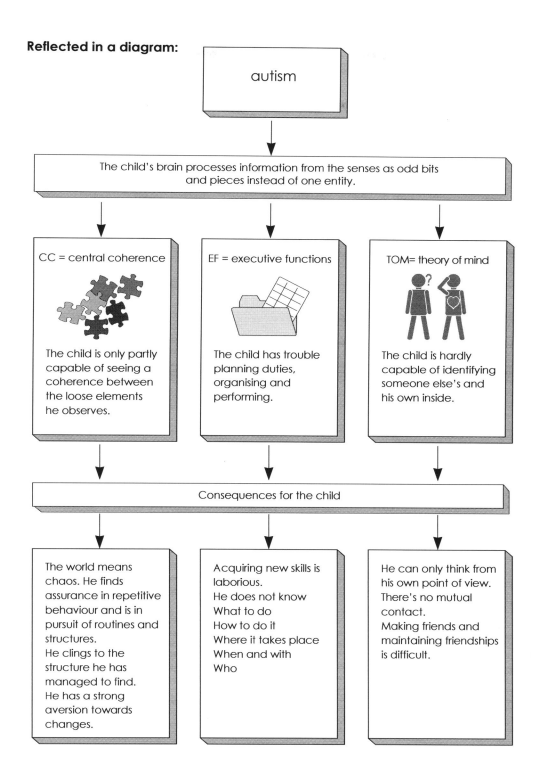

autism

The child's brain processes information from the senses as odd bits and pieces instead of one entity.

CC = central coherence

The child is only partly capable of seeing a coherence between the loose elements he observes.

EF = executive functions

The child has trouble planning duties, organising and performing.

TOM= theory of mind

The child is hardly capable of identifying someone else's and his own inside.

Consequences for the child

The world means chaos. He finds assurance in repetitive behaviour and is in pursuit of routines and structures.
He clings to the structure he has managed to find.
He has a strong aversion towards changes.

Acquiring new skills is laborious.
He does not know
What to do
How to do it
Where it takes place
When and with
Who

He can only think from his own point of view.
There's no mutual contact.
Making friends and maintaining friendships is difficult.

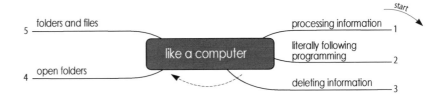

5 folders and files

processing information 1 _start_

like a computer

literally following programming 2

4 open folders

deleting information 3

4 Like a computer

When you deal with children with autism every day, you notice that the way their minds work is similar to how a computer works. Making this comparison allows us to better understand and instruct the child. Which does not mean we want to downgrade the child to a machine! Our objective is to better understand the child and – after a while – finding more 'handles' for the child's upbringing.

computer
as a tool

The child does not sense what he is expected to do in some situations, how his behaviour should be, what he should say or do. Parents very much want their children to take part in society. You can do that by 'programming' his everyday routine, giving him as many rules, appointments and step-by-step plans as possible. By introducing rules and subsequent actions in part, you provide him with 'survival programmes'. The child saves these data in so-called 'folders and files.' This is how he learns how to behave in a socially accepted manner. The child really wants to participate in this world and yearns to feel accepted. The rules saved will determine his behaviour, and his environment will be more positive. The more rules, the more grip: the better he feels.

Similarities between a 'brain folder' and a computer folder are:

- a 'brain folder' stands for data which were saved.
- everything the child knows is stored into different folders.
- you can help the child by adding a new folder - What should the child do? How, Where, When and with Who? - thus 'programming' him.
- perception is saved literally, meaning that if the pieces of the puzzle of perception are put together wrongly, saving the perception will go wrong, too.
- the child thinks along straight lines and can only see con nections which have been stored in a literal manner. He cannot see the connection on his own.
- he can only find a file, stored within a folder, if all the details are coherent with his saving method.

4.1 Processing information

As a result of his disorder, a child with autism processes information systematically. Only after having put the pieces of the puzzle together he can save this information. This means things should not proceed too quickly and the coherence must be clear. Similar situations show different details, often causing the child to recognise this coherence much later, after many repetitions.

Saving - or storing - information works as follows: a new folder containing new data is created. Files which pertain to the new rule as well as 'exception files' are saved in this folder. The more evident the rule is established, the easier it will be for the child to carry it out. The more he practises a rule, the more he will be confronted with exceptions to it. If these exceptions are added to the file in which the rule has been saved, the child's reactions will become more and more flexible.

data are saved in separate folders

Below are a few simple examples of how a computer works compared to how the brain of a child with autism works in saving data:

4.2 Literally following programming

Children with autism benefit from 'good programming'. Just like a computer has been programmed with certain data, a child with autism will almost 'automatically' perform the rules established between you and him (q.v. Chapter 4 and 5).

Olivia (7) has been taught - after some training - to open her bedroom curtains in the morning, before she goes downstairs. She never forgets. She also opens them when they shouldn't be open (e.g. because of the cold), because she is merely following her 'programming'.

After a play afternoon in the schoolyard the children go back in to collect their stuff, preparing to leave, but Amber (11) takes out her books and gets to work. The other children make fun of her: 'We're going home, school's over!' But Amber has learned that 'going inside' means 'getting back to work'.

Folder

Files & exceptions

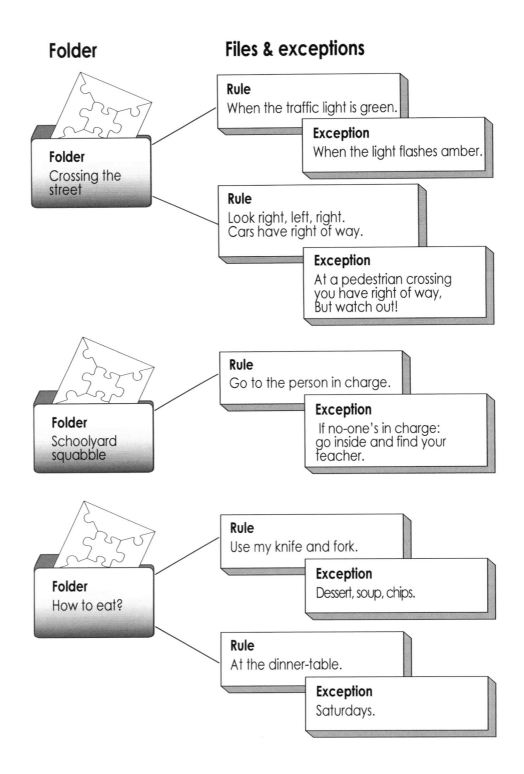

Folder
Crossing the street

Rule
When the traffic light is green.

Exception
When the light flashes amber.

Rule
Look right, left, right.
Cars have right of way.

Exception
At a pedestrian crossing
you have right of way,
But watch out!

Folder
Schoolyard squabble

Rule
Go to the person in charge.

Exception
If no-one's in charge:
go inside and find your
teacher.

Folder
How to eat?

Rule
Use my knife and fork.

Exception
Dessert, soup, chips.

Rule
At the dinner-table.

Exception
Saturdays.

Because children with autism can be thus programmed, they memorise things very well and have no problem recounting information on subjects such as number plates, dates of birth, facts about volcanoes, electrical engineering etc. Once saved, data just roll out as soon as the folder is opened. (Which, by the way, may serve them well later in life).

On the other hand they may handle the saved data quite rigidly. For example:

Eric has learned to: pee, wash his hands and sit down at the table. If occasionally there's no water at his disposal then there is a big problem. Eric gets stuck: his environment does not fit his programme, which he has to go through step-by-step.

4.3 Deleting information
Deleting information works similar to programming. In a child with autism, a folder which has been created can be deleted fairly easily again. For example by drawing its contents and drawing a large red cross across it, at the same time making the following agreement: 'We no longer use this.'

It is important to remember that this works only if a new folder is created with another advisable rule. An undesirable folder (e.g. swearing or calling names) may be deleted and replaced by a new one containing other advisable information.

Often, Michael (7) has trouble falling asleep at night. He gets out of bed explaining his head is 'just so full.' Wishing to clarify what he means exactly, we ask Michael to make a drawing of what is inside his head. Michael starts drawing his head and describes the songs he has to memorise and the duties he has to perform.
It is obvious that it is difficult for Michael to think and at the same time write down what he is saying. That is why the counsellor takes over. The entire drawing simply brims over with the fullness of Michaels head. 'There isn't even room left for a dream,' is how he puts it. Michael cannot conclude things but his mind stays busy all the time.

changes in routines confuse the child

combine deleting folders with creating new ones containng advisable information

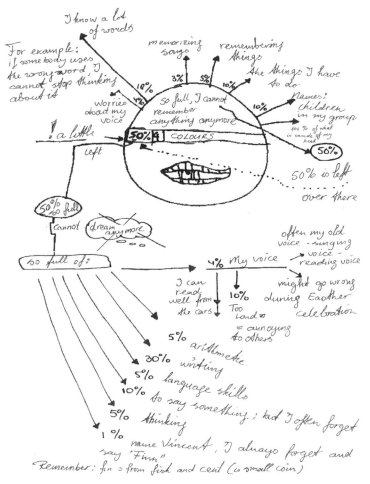

I know a lot of words

For example: if somebody uses the wrong word, I cannot stop thinking about it

memorizing songs — 3%

remembering things — 5%

the things I have to do — 10%

So full, I cannot remember anything anymore

Worries about my voice

! a little left

50% COLOURS

names: children in my group — 10%

100% of what is inside of my head

50%

50% is left over there

50% too full

Cannot dream anymore

So full of:

4% My voice

often my old voice - singing voice - reading voice

I can read well from the cars

10% Too Loud = annoying to others

might go wrong during Easter celebration

5% arithmetic

30% writing

5% language skills

10% to say something: but I often forget

5% thinking

1% name Vincent, I always forget and say "Finn"

Remember: fin = from fish and cent (is small coin)

In order to give Michaels school things a 'place of their own', Michael is given a loose-leaf folder in which he can put all the things from his head onto paper – split up into categories. This helps him to release things 'in his head' and not having to memorise everything all the time. At school he is allowed to keep the paper close at hand: it contains lyrics, reading, writing and arithmetic rules, other pupils' names including photographs and memory aids. Every now and then Michael is assigned to a low arousal spot, where he can do his work. Michael has found another solution to conclude unpleasant things that have taken place at school: he makes a drawing of them and hides it in the sandbox. A drawback is that people can walk across it. Together with Michael we are looking for a more practical solution.

Michael creates a folder on the computer in which he can put things that occupy him, allowing him to put these issues literally 'out of his head'. By deleting them from the computer he deletes them altogether.

4.4 Open folders

A folder which is not closed, remains open. In his head, the child continues to be occupied by the subject and can go on asking the same questions, performing the same actions or bringing up the same topics of conversation for hours, days or even years. If this is disturbing to the child and/or his environment, you can put an end to this behaviour by closing off the folder. This requires clarifying its contents, deleting the old issues in cooperation with the child, substituting them with new stuff.

A seven-year-old who cannot stop talking about firework and cannot wait for New Year's Eve all year long, gets disturbed, and so does his environment. You can stop this undesirable behaviour by saying: 'Stop, you are going to stop talking about this now.' But remember to always create a new folder containing things which are permitted. The rule in this folder could be: 'When the toy shop brochure with firework comes in - which is just before Christmas - then you can start talking about firework again.' You have in fact deleted the folder which contained his way of looking at firework, at the same time creating a new deal about the moment opening the folder again.

open folders are bothering him

Some children with autism have 'stims': items or subjects in which they show an extreme interest. They use such an item for repetitive behaviour such as spinning around a saucer or winding a bit of string around their fingers or, like Charlie, holding a little rake. A stim can also be something the child wants to talk about every day. At times when the world appears unclear to him, he will use his stim as a means to feel safe.

stims

4.5 Folders and files

I have noticed that creating folders - both for and together with the child - will help him tremendously in holding out in our society which has so many unwritten laws and rules. The more folders containing rules and step-by-step plans a child will have created, the easier it will be for him to cope.
Over and over again I consider the question: how will I teach him this, in this way, or in a different way? And I keep wondering: will I not make him too rigid if I teach him this in this way? Could there be a more flexible form, which he can handle as well? Does this rule fit his environment as well? It is a cost-benefit analysis, for the child as well as for the parent. Do I have the energy to teach the child like this? Do I postpone it? Or do I pick a simpler solution?

Reflecting upon appropriate folders and files requires a great effort from parents or attendants. Folder contents must be 100% in order, or else the child won't understand and will give up. Folders create a sense of space inside the child's head: this is how it is. He does not have to think about it. From our point of view this would naturally mean restraint but for the child with autism it means a framework allowing him to broaden his horizons.

Parents often worry that a stranger will snatch their child from the street. I always advise them to create a folder - together with the child - containing the following rule: 'When I'm out on the street, I can get into a car only if Mummy, Daddy, Granny (and so on) are in it.' The exception will be: 'You can also get into a car if Mummy has told you beforehand that someone else will come and pick you up.' The child will be performing this rule rigidly. It may very well be that he will not get into the neighbour's car, if the neighbour offers him a ride because of the pouring rain. The child will not renounce the rule. If a neighbour comes to pick him up from school because Mummy is feeling sick, he will not go with her. In this case, the exception to the rule will be that Mummy calls him and tells him to go with the neighbour because Mummy is not feeling well. For the child now this will be in line again with the rule you agreed upon. In any case, you can rest assured that the child will never come along with a stranger.

The longer the child will use folders, the more exception files folders will contain, the more flexible he becomes. The fact that folder contents never change will give him grip.

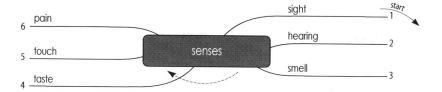

5 Senses

A child with autism can either be hypersensitive or hyposensitive in his sensory observations. This differs from child to child. It is very important to hear from the child if it is bothering him. This can strongly determine his reactions and sometimes have a major impact on family life. The child is incapable of changing it, but can learn how to better deal with it.

5.1 Sight

The child's eyes may be hypersensitive, meaning that he is overwhelmed by incoming stimuli. The huge amount of puzzle pieces simply gets too dominant. He covers his eyes, trying to cut himself off from all those stimuli. Preparing him for things that will happen and naming what he observes, will help him put the puzzle pieces together quicker. The child can make fleeting eye contact. As described earlier, the child can do only one thing at a time. If he has to look someone in the eye, this may give him so many stimuli that, next to it, he is incapable of listening (or obeying).

Danny (15), pre-university education: 'When I look into your eyes, that's unnecessary information to me. It will keep me from doing what I am doing. I'd rather not look at you so I can go on thinking.'

Never enforce eye contact. You and the child can agree that if he is talking to someone, for the sake of politeness he will focus his look somewhere on the face of the person he's talking to (e.g. between the eyes). In that way he does not really have to look the other person in the eye. When you talk to him, you can take into account your position (sit next to the child instead of facing him) and you can have a conversation with the help of writing paper. In this way eye contact can be partly avoided. If you deliberately make less (long) eye contact, there will be more space for his own thoughts.

5.2 Hearing

Hypersensitive ears in autistic children is more common than we think. Just imagine you are watching video-recordings of a party you taped earlier. All sounds have entered the microphone equally loud and are on tape. When you attended that party, you could push irrelevant sounds to the background. A child with autism cannot distinguish between main issues and side issues. All sounds, whether they are relevant or not, enter his ears equally loud. If you want to know if this is the case in your child, ask yourself the following questions:

- Can the child hear really well? (For example: when he is upstairs, he can hear what is being said downstairs)
- Do loud noises bother him?
- Can he not stand the loud music his brother or sister plays, whereas he plays his own music at least equally loud?
- Does he sometimes cover his ears?
- Does he indicate pain when you whisper in his ear?
- Does he seem deaf from time to time?
- At parties, does he hear only noise? Is it hard for him to turn off background noise, making it difficult for the relevant sounds to 'arrive'?

Mark avoids rooms with a fridge or freezer. Nobody understands why. Until it turns out that the hum of these devices is a great nuisance to him. This is so disturbing for him that he can no longer understand what is being said. Mark is the only one who can hear the humming, and he is unable to shut it out.

5.3 Smell

In your opinion, the child may demonstrate an exaggerated reaction to 'smells': he regularly comments on smells of e.g. food, other people or money. It may well be that he can smell excessively well and these smells really bother him. He is then swamped by what he experiences as a nasty smell. The only thing he can do at that moment is smell. You will see him put down everything else and hear and see his exaggerated reactions to the smell.

Sometimes the smell has to be taken away because it literally makes the child vomit or because it cannot put it in perspective. The latter is something you can learn the child, e.g. by saying: 'That dung smell comes with the farm, let's not talk about it. If you think about it, keep it inside your head. Other people don't want to hear about it.' This has to be repeated for some time, but after a while he will have made a folder for this one, too. If the child thinks out loud, you can hear him say to himself: 'It stinks, but it comes with the farm!' By putting things into perspective the child is capable of conquering his nasty smell problem.

hearing

smell

5.4 Taste

Mouth hypersensitivity can cause the child to have trouble eating e.g. hot food, solid chunks, hot and cold food simultaneously, or a certain substance that makes him retch. Presenting different kinds of food apart from each other or using a sectioned (toddler) plate can be a solution. A toothbrush in the mouth can cause similar issues. Brushing teeth following a step-by-step plan (available at your Area Health Authority or dentist) can make things so predictable that the retching will diminish. Also, mint toothpaste can be the source of big problems.

Next to eating and talking, the child is faced with tasting and feeling in his mouth. At that moment of time, all his senses are hyperactive and the child has to puzzle very hard in order to get all the information processed.

What strikes one most, is that some children have not learned How to chew. Jamie, for example, bites his food twice and then swallows it. Jamie has yet to learn How to chew.

5.5 Touch

Most autistic children like being touched only if they ask for it themselves, not when you feel like touching them. Patting the child's back or stroking his head can be experienced as something unpleasant. Especially an unexpected approach from behind can give him a fright.

At mealtimes, Lilly (11) is seated next to her mother. Every time her mother fetches something from the kitchen, Lilly clasps her leg behind the leg of her mother's chair, so she cannot sit down. This has been going on for months, despite many at-tempts by the parents to end this conduct. Lilly cannot indicate why she does this. Mother has become so fed up that by now she snatches the chair away violently, but still Lilly won't give up. Mother decides to move to the other side of the table. This change clearly pleases Lilly.

Unconsciously, Lilly chooses to rule out a sensory experience, namely the fact that physical proximity troubles her. Because the table is rather small, Mother is seated close to Lilly. When she is having her meal, she is unable to deal with other stimuli: she is literally over-excited. She has to be looking, smelling, hearing and tasting already, so she does not want to deal with the addition of (an unexpected) touch. So, it does not have to do with Mother personally but merely the processing of too much (sensory) information.

5.6 Pain

Autistic children do feel pain (or other physical symptoms) but their experience may be less intense than in persons without autism. Apart from this, it can sometimes be hard for them to phrase their pain, because (the right) words are failing.

This means their environment cannot properly respond, or is late in responding, which sometimes means the child goes to school while he is ill.

At school, Lisa breaks her arm. This is not discovered by her parents until the evening, when she has been home for hours, because she cannot indicate pain herself.

On the other hand, the very same child can be seized by panic at the sight of a tiny drop of blood, because he is afraid to bleed to death or because blood has a distinct colour which does not belong there. After all, you cannot see an arm is broken, but you can see blood.

The same goes for stools. In my work I have regularly encountered children with toilet-training or constipation issues or problems emptying their bowels, all with a dual cause: first of all not recognising body signals or inability to phrase them (this bellyache means I need to go), and secondly not being able to survey the subsequent actions (for example: walking, going to toilet, putting on light, pulling down trousers, turning around and sit down. What must I do and How?). If parents know at an early stage that their child is autistic, these problems – if not of a medical nature - can be anticipated.

I first visited Harry's (special school) parents when he was twelve years old. During the day Harry's trousers were always a little soiled, but the actual 'poo event' was a daily drama which had to be planned around all the other obligations and activities. Apart from this, he had a lot of bellyaches and obstipation symptoms. Harry did not indicate himself when he had to go. There was no fixed moment for doing a poo, either. At my advice the parents set up an evening ritual. What comes before and after the pooping, is the same every day, which means that the pooping always takes place at a certain point in time. In planning this, the parents have stuck to the moment of Harry's - supposed - natural stool as much as possible. I asked questions about the 'stool process' up until that moment, noticing that toilet-paper made Harry's flesh creep. It turned out that he also did not want to wipe his nose with Kleenex and

had an aversion to kitchen paper and paper napkins. It turned out that Harry had an oversensitive skin reaction to paper in that form. So it was decided to let Harry use wet toilet-paper from that day on. We told Harry that there would be changes and after they were carried out, he started emptying his bowels at the agreed moment of time after only a few days.

The bellyache problems and planning of the 'poo event' became things of the past once and for all.

We went a little further during our next visit. Dad always wiped Harry's buttocks which still made him person-dependent. Now that the toilet-paper problem had been tackled, Harry was capable of wiping his own buttocks. The question was: what does he need for that? We agreed that Dad would start teaching him certain operations (structure dependability) which involved: wiping his buttocks three times with wet toilet-paper after bowel motion, turn around, flush and take a shower. Harry picked this up smoothly, too.

Harry's example is, again, a matter of predictability (about when he is allowed to answer the call of nature) and clearness with the help of 'The Essential 5' (What he should do, How, Where, When and with Whom). A distinct daily structure (visualized by means of visual aids or flash cards) can often solve 'doing a poo' issues as well.

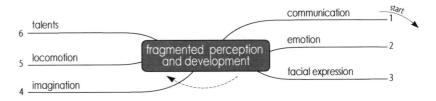

6 Development

Autism is a pervasive developmental disorder, which means that all developmental areas are affected. Therefore, the consequences of autism can be seen and recognised in everything the child does. The child will always be autistic, but it depends on the barcode and the clearness and predictability of his environment if and when he is bothered by it.

6.1 Communication

There is such a substantial difference between the way we communicate with autistic children – the language the child uses – and the way we usually communicate that miscommunication arises easily. It is very important for us to understand the child's language so we can fine-tune our communication and usage, for he often does not understand our language because of his autism. We will have to learn to gear to his manner of understanding. This is so essential that chapters 9 to 13 have been reserved for communication and autism.

6.2 Emotion

Children with autism have trouble recognising their own emotions. Their defective 'theory of mind' causes them to have little idea about their own wishes, needs, opinions and emotions. Having no words or too few words for those, they do not know how to express themselves.

Sean, who is totally into tractors, says: 'I love that tractor so much… I am feeling hearts in my stomach!'

Noah (10) has been called names. It is explained to him that there are feelings inside of him and that is the reason why another person cannot call him names. So now he has learned that there are feelings inside of him. He puts this notion in a new folder which is connected to calling names. When someone is abusing him now, he invariably produces the phrase: 'I have feelings, so you cannot call him names.' The actual abuse does not seem to hurt him, but everything has to pass off according to the learned rule.

Apart from this, Noah is told that the other person did not feel anything when he was doing that. Noah takes this literally and adds this information to the folder of the abusive person: it is someone without feelings. This is how he put it into a drawing:

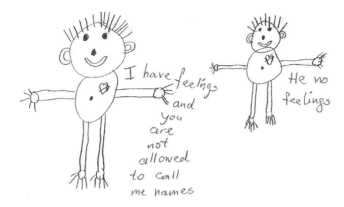

Children with autism are different from other children in expressing their emotions. They are incapable or hardly capable of responding, or react only in a very extreme manner. It looks as if they do not know where to draw the line. When a child talks it takes the observed facts - which are the sum of details - as a starting-point. Emotions stay in the background.
It is difficult to concretize how feelings should be expressed in a proper manner, because most people simply sense this.

consequences
for emotions

Roan, who is very enthusiastic, is unable to soften the loudness of his voice: he can be heard everywhere. An agreement is made that he can talk just as loudly as the people around him. This rule helps him soften his voice.

Many autistic children show almost no facial expression to express their feelings. That does not mean that the child does not have feelings: it does, but uses a different means to express them. Because this is unique in every child, parents must go and look for the means in which their child expresses his emotions.

Justin (12), Year 6 primary school, is given the assignment to write a poem about being in love. He has never been in love, does not know what it feels like and what it implies. But there is one thing he knows for sure: he never wants to fall in love, because having a girlfriend costs money. In order to comply with the assignment he writes the following:

41

Not yet not ever
Being in love seems funny to me
because you look at each other
all the time
I have never been in love
Which seems wonderfull to me

The idea of being in love
Is not very appealling to me
Often things must be done secretly
To me, it seems great to not be in love

For Justin, being in love is nothing more than looking at each other. He cannot imagine anything else. Because of his defective TOM, he does not have any feelings when it comes to girls.

Children with autism often have difficulty recognising other people's emotions and responding in an appropriate manner. They have a limited ability to enter into their own inner self and put themselves in someone else's shoes, which means it is difficult for them to take into account that other person's feelings. This, too, varies from child to child. Not every child finds it equally hard to take into account another person's feelings (bear in mind the barcode).

consequences
for emotions

In the course of life, understanding and feeling cannot be increased. But it is possible to teach a child with autism how to respond to certain emotions, so it may look as if there is real empathy. This will often look a bit stiff and unnatural, but is to be preferred above an incorrect response or no reaction at all. Chapter 21 'appointment notebook' tells you how to teach him rules for this.

Mother is ill, but is trying hard to keep going. Lilly (11) notices that things do not take their regular course, gets upset and starts being a nuisance. Mother expects her 'big daughter' to help out a bit, but the opposite is the case. No matter what she does to make clear to Lilly to be cooperative, nothing helps. In the afternoon, Mother breaks down and installs herself on the sofa with a blanket.

When Lilly sees this, she asks: 'Are you ill?' When Mother says 'yes', Lilly jumps up and comes back a little later with a nice tray of tea, biscuits and fruit. Lilly is not able to recognise illness until she sees someone lying down covered by a blanket. This is when she can exhibit appropriate behaviour. When Mother is ill but keeps walking around, Lilly is unable to recognise Mother is ill. Lilly has a folder in her head ('this is what being ill looks like') and cannot act until all conditions are met.

6.3 Facial expression

A child with autism has trouble understanding facial expressions. Because he does not understand the underlying emotions, only the sum of the details of the facial expressions. can give him clues. Eyebrows, mouth and eyes: they all provide information, but this varies from person to person. As a matter of fact, people all express emotions like anger, sadness, fear, happiness, disappointment and so on in a different way. This makes it impossible for many autistic children to learn how to recognize facial expressions. Chaos is completed if somebody says something which does not match his facial expressions (e.g. looking seriously when making a joke).

Amir (15, Higher General Secondary School) wants to go through the door but Olivia is blocking his way. He asks politely: "Please let me pass", to which Olivia says 'no', stepping aside simultaneously. Amir is totally upset, gets angry and asks: "Why are you stepping aside?" Saying no but 'doing yes' is very confusing for him, because he does not understand the joke. Luckily, Olivia understands she has been ambiguous and offers her apologies: "I'm sorry, Amir, I was wrong. I meant 'yes'". For Amir the puzzle pieces now fall into place; things are again as they should be and Olivia can be trusted again.

Sometimes it is advisable to say certain things for the in order have to decide to say certain things for the child's reassurance, so that the world is alright again.

6.4 Imagination

Children with autism have a hard time imagining things which are not tangibly present. What you can't see, simply isn't there, seems to be the idea sometimes.

Tanya (9) denies outright that the poo in the toilet is hers. She has not seen it come out, so it is not hers!

consequences for facial expression

what you can't see, isn't there

When the child comes home from school, it may well be that he has little to recount. He is at home now, isn't he? School? What are you talking about? The imaginative powers to go back in one's mind are insufficient. The child lives here and now. Therefore, looking for lost items can be a major problem, too. It is impossible to imagine walking the road back or imagining a place different from the one you are now.

The best thing to do is talking to these children in the 'here and now', meaning to talk about where you are now, what is taking place and what is visible right now. Do not talk about things which are not there. Should you decide to do so, go to the place where the topic of conversation took place. Draw or act out what took place, preferably as true to life as possible. This will increase the chances that he will be able again to open the folder in which the information was saved.

In Eric's (11) reading comprehension lesson it says that the mouse in the elevator is gone. The man in the elevator makes funny dancing movements, keeping the opening of a trouser-leg closed. Near his knee is a small lump. Where is the mouse? Eric's answer is: 'gone'. Of course it is true that the text literally says that the mouse is gone, but Eric does not have the imagination to understand the rest of the story. He makes no connection between the man dancing and keeping the trouser-leg closed and the disappearance of the mouse.

consequences
for reading
comprehension

Malik goes to summercamp. He has been told beforehand that they will go camping one night and what the plans are every day. Also, the division into groups has been made known. Before they leave, the children are asked to make a drawing of the camp. Malik draws grass, flowers, sun and sky. Without having seen the real situation he cannot imagine what the camp must look like. And he does not have the imagination to imagine a tent, even though he has gone camping before.

consequences for drawing

For some children with autism, all details must match the image they have stored in their folder. If one tiny detail deviates, they will not recognize the object or situation as such causing them to display inappropriate behaviour.

Tim (12), special school, always puts on his own clothes. One day, he refuses to do so. Mother has removed part of his zip off pants because the weather is nice and sunny. Just because one tiny detail is different, Tim does not recognize the situation. He gets so confused that he is unable to swing into action.

consequences for everyday matters

Autistic children are often visual thinkers: for them, words are more difficult to understand than images and pictures. Apart from this, words are volatile. As soon as they have been uttered, they are gone. Words must be turned into images in their heads first before they can give meaning to them - in order to take action. This is why it is easier for the child to understand what you are talking about if he can see what you are saying. Apart from children with autism who lack imaginative powers or imagination, there are others who seem to have too much of it. Often this applies only to his special field of interest.

visual thinking instead of thinking in words

At the end of the school year, Joshua (8), Year 3 primary school and his class visit their new teacher for an hour. They have already been assigned the places which they will occupy after the summer holidays. The teacher tells things and reads to them. Back in their own classroom, the children are asked to draw their new classroom. All that Joshua does, is draw four tables, four chairs and four children, in a corner of the sheet. But his imagination fills the whole sheet of paper with self-invented comic characters.
Joshua does have imagination, but when he is asked what the rest of the classroom looks like, his imaginative powers abandon him. Because of his jigsaw puzzle observation he needed much more time to take in the entire classroom. Now he has just managed to remember the group he was in.

consequences for imaginative powers

Joshua creates his own comics, including his own heroes. Not understanding reality or not knowing things makes him insecure. It feels much safer to use his imagination to fill the gaps. It's better to live with predictable things - his own imaginative heroes - than with insecurity or ignorance.

Sometimes it is hard for children to distinguish between imagination and reality. It is best to shield them from TV programmes with an unrealistic representation of reality because they can take it literally, causing an incorrect image of real life.

Mia (16) watches a soap opera on TV in which one of the leading stars changes boyfriends regularly. Mia thinks this is normal and tries very hard to do so herself. With all its consequences.

Ralph (11), special education, has a new game. His mother - happy to see him indulge in fantasies - is eager to participate at first. Ralph has a friend: an imaginary cat. It visits Ralph every now and then and can only be seen by him.
Initially, this fantasy is fun, but soon Ralph's life is taken over by the cat. He has to beat everyone else because the cat says so. He can never ever lose a game again, only from his cousin because he's family. The cat pays nightly visits causing Ralph to stay awake and not getting enough sleep. At night the cat orders him to do things. At that time Ralph turns into a cat himself. He shows his hairy arms to Mum and gets very angry when she says she cannot see the hair: for in his perception it is the truth. This situation has been going on for half a year now. Ralph is getting more and more tired, which causes his mother to ask for advice.
Our assumption is that this situation has to do with Ralph's autism, in which case Mum can close the cat's folder, preparing Ralph beforehand. She hands him another new folder which states how the rules will be from this moment on. Mum defines this, without consulting Ralph, and tells him so directively (meaning: friendly but very decisively). It is agreed that tonight the cat will visit for the last time. It will then give its last orders and leave, never to come back again. Together with Ralph, Mum creates a new folder. The new agreement is that, starting tomorrow, Ralph will be a boy again all day and all night. A boy who will go to bed at 8.30 until 7 o'clock the next morning. After that night, the cat never comes back again.

6.5 Locomotion

Somewhat stiff walking and running typify the locomotion of many children with autism. (Subsequently, quite a number of children with autism get physiotherapy). On the other hand, some of these children are quite supple in other movements.

Alice walks and runs like Pinocchio. But she dances just as graciously as a ballerina.

Some children have mastered something and the next moment they seem to have lost the hang of it. This may be a result of an altered detail.

Stephen stands out because he can ride his bike very well. But after a while he seems to have forgotten how to do it.

6.6 Talents

Many children with autism can observe details astonishingly well and have very clear memories. Their knowledge of facts and details can really astound us. De facto this is very reliable information, but one cannot totally rely on coherence and understanding. They tell us their own truth, which is not necessarily the truth.

Still, the child is not lying. For being able to lie means to be able to predict the other person's reaction and bending the truth in order to avoid a dreaded reaction. Their mere inability to lie provides these children with honesty: a much-valued quality.

Children with autism like things that are constant. This is why they often know the alphabet and numbers at an early age. They love clocks. Some children even know the railway timetable by heart.

Elliott (12) has a wonderful memory. He remembers exactly every birthday present he has been given - and the person who gave it - since his third birthday.

Many children with autism are hypersensitive in all their senses. This means they have a greater perception than other children, causing them to be bothered by things which would not trouble an ordinary child. But this can also have a positive effect. This quality allows the child to enjoy music, beautiful colours or movements immensely and become totally absorbed.

Frederick is not able to read music, but he can repeat by ear complex music made by others and does so faultlessly, and with a great sense of rhythm.

consequences for locomotion

jigsaw puzzle observation results in: having a very clear memory, factual knowledge and honesty

observing details

sensory hypersensitivity

7 Auti-specs

In regular upbringing parents follow their child's development and react to it as they (intuitively) think it is best. Parents enjoy their children and guide them. Parents and educators of autistic children have long since found out that, in the case of their child, regular upbringing skills do not work. Parents are required to look at the child's behaviour from a different angle: knowledge-based observation.

If, after having read the previous chapters, you have learned that the smallest of changes can put the child's brain off balance, you can also learn to see this. You can learn to see that the child is thinking, you can see him hesitate. His eyes tell you that he is temporarily losing track of the situation. More and more you learn how to look from this child's perspective, and from the perspective of his disorder.

put on your

!!

If you can put yourself in his shoes, it means a world of difference. You learn to see whenever his brain gets upset, when too many puzzle pieces must be put together. These facts are reflected only by his behaviour. It is the only way to express himself. He has difficulty phrasing his emotions. If he gets stuck and does not know anymore how to make things clear, that is when undesirable behaviour comes into being. Therefore, this kind of behaviour is a direct result of his environment being unclear and unpredictable.

So: put on your auti-specs and look at the child again, using this knowledge. And see what it is he needs from you. Which is: the introduction of cohesion. This requires an adjustment of your communication. Fulfilling both conditions allows him to develop and grow further. How you can do this, is explained in the next section.

7.1 Applying auti-specs

Autism isn't something that shows up every now and then. Autism is always there. In every situation, a child with autism has to put the puzzle pieces together. He cannot see the big picture, he cannot put himself in someone else's shoes and he cannot organize very well. This does not imply that every situation is equally troubling to the child. The clearer, calmer and more predictable the situation, the easier it is for the child to cope with his autism.

Only when bothered by it, he is impaired. Teaching him survival strategies makes him less dependent and therefore less impaired.

It is up to the adult to put on auti-specs and learn how to look and interpret. How is he dealing with this situation? Is it working? Are things clear enough? Is there something I should clarify? The more clearness and predictability the child's environment contains, the less he feels impaired. The more he can grow and develop. Presenting him an overall picture by means of structures and handing him rules makes it easier for him to keep going. Consequently it is a little easier for him to cope with a changing world. Hereafter we will show you how he can be guided towards increasing self-reliance.

7.2 Knowledge-based observation and education

To be well tuned in, it is important to recognize the disorder in the child's behaviour. Every child can be a nuisance from time to time, which most of the time is a result of normal development. But in a child with autism it is a result of the disorder. It is very important to make a distinction between these two things.

A grown-up person having this knowledge and looking at a child with autism understands the consequences of the disorder for the child. One could say he observes the child through auti-specs, thus helping the child to clarify his world. This requires knowledge about his way of thinking, feeling, communication and acting, making you see more and more characteristics belonging to the disorder and unique to the child. You learn to understand what the disorder means to him. When a child with autism does something wrong, it is usually not done from unwillingness or to spite you: it is mere impotence.

If only the negative behaviour is tackled, the underlying cause does not change and the problem persists. In the case of autistic children, actions of the environment should expressly not target on tackling the negative behaviour itself (e.g. physical or verbal violence, kicking, calling names, slapping, head banging, being introvert or obtrusive, demonstrating compulsive or claiming behaviour) and not on tackling psychosomatic symptoms either (bellyache, headache) or on symptoms such

if you put on your auti-specs you can enter into his mind and, starting from there, see what he needs

as refusing to work, ignoring others, demonstrating incorrect reactions as well as stool, eating and sleeping issues. What needs to be dealt with, are the underlying causes of this behaviour and the following: unclearness and unpredictability. For the child, all above-mentioned matters are his way of saying: 'Help me! Tell me how things work!'

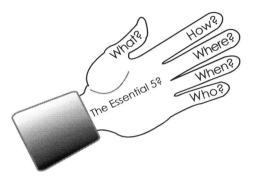

As a result of his autistic disorder, the child has difficulty asking for help. For: What should he tell Who? When he feels unhappy it is because the world is an incomprehensible chaos to him. The only way to make this clear is through his behaviour. So you should 'translate' all this negative behaviour into a cry for clearness and predictability.

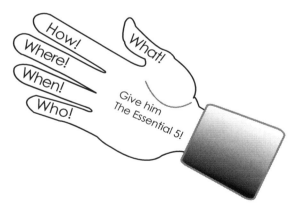

Parents can provide this using 'The Essential 5', meaning both the child's request and the parent's offer. At work I can see parents recounting these five points on their fingers until this method has become familiar to them.

8 Coherence via 'The Essential 5'

Because the child thinks differently and his jigsaw puzzle observation affects his entire development, it is the environment that needs to make adjustments. The child's brain processes things observed in fragments and the child is doing its utmost to see the cohesion between those fragments. For everyday life this means that it is difficult for the child to make connections between all the impressions he gets. He is impaired if, for example, he cannot see cause and result and if he fails to notice relationships between people. He does not understand what topography has to do with holidays and why he suddenly needs to wear a summer coat, when he has been comfortable in his warm winter coat all winter.

Every child must feel safe in order to develop properly. Being able to see the big picture gives a sense of (fundamental) security. Apart from nourishment, clothing and having a roof over your head, feeling safe is a vital necessity for every human being (A.H. Maslow, A Theory of Human Motivation, 1943). If this necessity is not satisfied, one cannot grow and develop any further; one is merely surviving instead of living. Therefore it is vitally important for the environment to create cohesion for autistic children who themselves are unable to see the big picture and as a result feel unsafe.

Often parents and educators of children with autism find out soon enough that regular upbringing methods do not work. Being punished, rewarded or praised usually do not teach the child to change his behaviour. Experience tells us that many behavioural problems vanish when cohesion is introduced in an autistic child's life, allowing him to perform tasks he did not do before. Could not do, I should say, really, because he was unable to see the coherence.

In today's complicated society, for us making connections between apparently odd fragments is difficult enough as it is. But for a child with autism, it can be totally impossible.

introduction
of coherence
for the child by
means of
'The Essential 5'

Wiping your bottom and doing a poo: they belong together. Someone who fails to see the connection between these actions will think little of performing them in the wrong order, or for example, omitting the latter action. He simply cannot see what one has to do with the other.

While working with parents and children it has become apparent to me that the basis of cohesion are these five points: What, How, When, Where and Who (and the environment should subsequently be clear and predictable about these five aspects). These '5' form the basis of this book in handling children with autism. By linking up tasks ('What') perfectly all the time, there is even more cohesion. Introducing cohesion is helping the child to make it easier to put the puzzle pieces together.

The child observes in jigsaw puzzle pieces and by replying in puzzle pieces you are linking up with his way of thinking. If you have a problem with the child, look at it as a puzzle you must solve, making use of 'The Essential 5'. This is the basis of this book which is an overall approach for the guidance of autistic children. By handling this puzzle correctly you can be very clear to the child, because you link up with his task-oriented way of thinking.

Many people have diaries to write down their appointments, sometimes adding extra information as a mnemonic. This allows you to see what has been agreed on. Because of their disorder, children with autism have an extra need for such an overview. This enables them to literally see the connections within the day or week, allowing them to understand which subsequent actions make up the 'What' (the thing(s) they have to do).

'The Essential 5' is a special type of diary, made to measure for autistic children. It is much more detailed than the diary you use yourself.

In this book I use the model of the puzzle instead of the diary model in order to link up well to the autistic child's needs. The four corner pieces of the What he must do are: How, Where, When and Who: they all provide grip in performing the What. They should contain the matching information and make the connections clear. Every item in the child's schedule is formed by an 'Essential 5', making his day an uninterrupted chain of tasks with every single task containing an 'Essential 5' which clarifies the What (he has to do).

The parent helps the child by means of ....

... *'The Essential 5'*

The meaning of every single puzzle piece is explained.
Together, the separate pieces support the What (the task).
*   What. Everything the child has to do (the task).
*   How. The way he must perform the task.
*   When. When does the task start and when will it be finished?
*   Where. At what location should the task be performed?
*   Who. Is he going to do it himself? What does the other person do?

These are the actual data the child needs in order to get going.

8.1 What

In this book, the What means everything the child has to do. Actions such as getting dressed, eating and making a puzzle, but also having a conversation, giving an answer, asking questions or asking for help. Waiting, transitions between one activity and the next, and listening are also part of the What. In short, everything the child must do, is called the What. The focus is on the What which is specified in the How, When, Where and Who.

What

Children with autism regard all activities as tasks which must be performed in a sequence. Generally speaking, they feel much more at ease if they know which tasks are still waiting to be performed rather than being left in the dark or having to make their own choices. When the child is idle, put him in the What; in other words: put him to work. (We also refer to this as 'put him in the task').

If the child with autism does everything as any other child, no action is required. No structure, no puzzle; he can do it independently, by himself. But if the child with autism cannot perform the What - a task - (well), the order in which the subsequent actions must be performed, is apparently unclear to him.

By consistently offering him things in the same order for a longer period of time, he learns to see the cohesion between subsequent actions. We put a ready-made puzzle in front of him, so to speak.

When he gets dressed, sometimes John has to put on his trousers first, but his shirt first on other occasions. It is of no relevance to his mother. But John gets frustrated because this way he never stops looking for coherence.

What

For the child, a task like getting dressed consists of a number of subsequent actions. Because of his jigsaw puzzle observation, it is important to teach him things in puzzle pieces as well, and to teach him the order in which the subsequent actions (puzzle pieces) take place. The introduction of a fixed order of tasks and subsequent actions is mandatory for the in-struction of children with autism.

We should realize that each subsequent action consists of 'The Essential 5', too. So, these subsequent actions must be made clear to the child one by one, by means of this 'The Essential 5'. The extent of subdivision differs from child to child; therefore the puzzle must be 'made to measure'.

The trick is to make the pieces he needs as big as possible, or as small as necessary, so he can continue to see the connections. This varies strongly from child to child, because it depends on three factors:

What
- the child's intellect;
- to what extent his autism is bothering him in this respect;
- the coherence which the child has already 'mastered' during the course of his life.

One child may want a rough overview, such as:
- 7.00: waking up;
- 7.05: getting up;
- 7.10: washing;
- 7.15: getting dressed;
- 7.30: breakfast.

But the other needs a more detailed overview:
- Mum calls me;
- Open duvet;
- Get up;
- Go to the toilet;
- Put fingers in trouser band;
- Pull down trousers;
- Sit down;
- Pee.

The trick is to find a balance between as few steps as possible on one hand, and as many steps as required for clarity's sake on the other hand.

8.2 How
The How stands for the way in which the What should be carried out. To us it is quite evident how things should be carried out, which is why you give no explanation most of the time. For a child with autism this is often too unclear. In order to get grip he needs more rules. If you explain the How of the What, he understands the game.

- Actions. Which actions should the child perform? In which order? How should the action be executed (for example using which knowhow or techniques)? Does he have the tools to perform the action (implements, aids)?
- Communication. How should he say or ask things? Using which words, which degree of politeness? How should he behave in this particular situation? Must he wait for his turn?

Simple examples of How.
- What: saying 'hello'. How do you do that? When you say hello, you look into the other person's eyes.
- What: sitting on a chair. How do you do that? Your legs are in front of you and you put your feet on the floor.
- What: eating chips. How? You use your fork to pin down your chips, you dip them into ketchup and put them in your mouth.
- What: taking a shower. That goes well. But How do you take a shower when you are having your period?

How

For a child with autism, it is the details that allow him to see the cohesion. And without that cohesion it is impossible for him to perform tasks. That is why it is vitally important to explain to the very last detail How he must do things. In the following example the How is not clear enough.

Mark can get very angry when he gets his Friday evening crisps. His parents do not know that it is very important to him How the bowl is filled. Sometimes it is filled to the brim, and it is a little less full on other occasions. For Mark this is too unpredictable and too unclear. It makes him feel secure when the amount of crisps is always exactly the same. So, Mark really wants to be informed about How his bowl of crisps looks.
His parents solve this problem as follows: he gets his own bowl with 'crisps' written on it, which he can fill up completely.
Full = full, something which is clear to Mark. From that moment on, he enjoys eating his crisps. And he knows beforehand How the bowl looks.

Mother tells Tim (3) to 'wave goodbye'. Tim does not respond. Mother says: 'Wave goodbye, Tim, with your hand.' Now Tim understands How he should do this and waves.

8.3 Where

In which place, in which room should the child perform his task? Often, a place is restricted to a particular task (e.g. toilet, bed, school) and this goes even stronger for a child with autism. Linking the What to a place hands him part of the coherence already. Two different things in the same spot (such as eating and working at school) can hamper the perception of the cohesion. This also happens when occasionally something is not in its usual place or something takes place in another location, which can make a mess of the cohesion acquired.

A fixed place (the Where) for a fixed task (the What) lends grip to the coherence. Therefore it can be difficult for a child to go to a 'strange' toilet.

Which requirements should a place have for a child with autism? The location must be clear and surveyable. Adapted to the child's needs. If the child is easily distracted by stimuli surrounding him, make sure that the surroundings are peaceful. This means more than 'less people around him'. Take a closer look at the walls, decoration, the way toys are stored or the organisation of the workplace. If this is too loud or chaotic, make adjustments that fit the need for survey and order.

For the organisation of toys nontransparent storage bins come in handy. The lid can be labelled with a drawing or visual aid of the contents.

How the What should be carried out, can be visualized with the Where. You could, for example, make photo place-mats for every family member to make clear everyone's position at the table.

The place-mats also show pictures of plates and cutlery to make it easier for the child to set the table by himself. Another example: put two small plastic containers on the work table. The left hand one has cards in it with What the child should do. After the child finishes a task, he puts the card upside down in the right hand container and starts the new task (which is now on top) in the left hand container.

8.4 When

In 'The Essential 5', the concept of 'time' (the When) can be interpreted quite literally, linked to the What. When does the What start and – just as important – when does it end? Children with autism take a big sense of security from time. Time lends clear cohesion to their day. Things taking place at fixed moments of the day, are daily recurrent certainties.

'I get up at 7.00, school starts at 8.30. School's over by 15.30 and I go home. I have my tea at 18.00. When Dad gets home, we go to football training.'

Alex (7) leaves his bed every night. When Mum goes on asking why, it emerges that on Friday evenings – when Dad is playing a sport and the little ones are asleep - he is allowed to come out of his bed and eat crisps cosily together with Mum. But Alex has no idea about what day of the week it is, so he leaves his bed every night of the week. His mother writes down on the calendar which day is Friday. From that moment on, Alex remains in his bed all other nights.

You can indicate the times 'on the clock' for him, depending on the child's needs, but also the order in which the What takes place. The order of things also belongs to the When, which is the reason this is often used in the so-called daily schedules used in crèches, nurseries and special education schools.

Experience teaches us that it is the free moments that yield problems, giving rise to the expression: 'Blank time = nuisance time'. Time in which the child has no task to perform, means lack of clarity which is very unpleasant for him, and he can even panic. You could say that his sensation is one of standing on quicksand. This may result in extremely obnoxious behaviour. He may either retreat into his own little world or take refuge in repetitive behaviour (stimming). Mostly, blank time occurs after school between 4 and 6 o'clock, when school ends early, on weekends and during holidays. Children expect the child to go and play, but a child with autism may lack the ability to get himself going. Planning time beforehand is helpful.

Blank time may also involve those 'just a few' minutes (no sooner have you turned around than your son gives his sister a wallop) or transitional moments between subsequent actions. These moments are annoying to the child, because at that particular moment it is not clear to him what he should be doing.

Mealtime is one of those moments which can be very tough: arguments can arise as a result of blank time.

Barry is at table with his parents and sister. After finishing his dinner, he looks around and sees that he is the first to have finished his food. He thinks out loud: 'Oh blimey, now I have to wait.' Because Barry knows full well that he can only leave the table after everyone else has finished eating. He figures out something to fill his time, asking his mother if he may leave the table and go to the toilet. But she thinks he should wait until dinner is over. Next, he asks for a glass of water. When he gets that, he drinks it excruciatingly slow – for no other reason than killing time.

Barry is very creative and is capable of finding his own solutions for the blank time giving him trouble. But many other children cannot manage, so that many a meal is messed up.

When a child knows about start time, but does not know when an activity ends, the following can happen:

The whole class is outside, singing for the principal's birthday. The teacher knows that for Sean waiting is very difficult. Which is why during the speech the teacher tells Sean to hold the tree. Sean is happy to comply. It gives him a task, filling in blank time. When the speech is over and class starts again, Sean is nowhere to be found. He is discovered still holding the tree: the teacher forgot to mention when the activity would end ('When the speech is over, you may go back to class').

Taking an order like 'Go and do something' is very hard for many of these children, because they need time to digest (jigsaw puzzle time). It is better to do it like this: 'In five minutes you go and put away your Lego, and then it is time for tea'. Or: 'After you have finished reading your comic, go and put your coat on the hallstand'.

Waiting is a problem, too. What is the What if you have to wait? Waiting is annoying as it is, but it is unbearable for a child with autism. He feels unsafe without the What. Whenever he has to wait, give him a task which matches the circumstances (e.g. counting cars, playing hopscotch, reading).

What follows after the What is also important to a lot of children. (Think of quicksand). This is when a new task starts. When the child requires so, clearly indicate which task (the What) you are referring to: this makes you predictable.

8.5 Who

A child with autism is often still dependent on people in his surroundings, making it vitally important to know who is the other person helping him, or what the other person is doing when he disappears from sight. 'What am I doing? Who is involved? What does the other do and is he doing that consistently?' Possibly the child wishes to know: 'Who can I turn to for help when I am performing this task?' It is not a matter of course for the child to go to the person on duty in case of a schoolyard incident; other children hear about this, and start using this option, too.

For many a child with autism it is important to know what the other person is doing when he has disappeared from sight, and when this important person will re-emerge. Picture this as follows: your 'film of tasks' separates itself from his. He can deal with this, as long as he knows when you will be back at his side. Make this concrete, linking it to time or a certain activity: this will give him clarity. For example: 'I am going downstairs now to answer the phone. When I am ready on the phone, I will come back to you.' Or: 'You go to sleep now. Mum and Dad will be downstairs drinking coffee and will go to bed as well at 10 o'clock. I will see you again when it's light outside.' I know a number of children who went to sleep simply because of the latter 'magical phrase', instead of lying and waiting for the parents to go to bed.

The child can also relate the What to a fixed person. When for a while Mum takes him to bed every night, he can be quite troublesome when Dad takes him to bed on another occasion. Sometimes, the child links one thing to another if it has occurred only once.

Josh gets a blow-up when Auntie comes to visit, and is quite a handful to Mum. It appears that the last time Auntie came to visit, she brought marshmallows. Josh is expecting marshmallows again this time around, but Auntie does not bring them. Josh is incapable of phrasing his expectations. But his negative behaviour plainly shows that something is wrong. This is because in his head he has put together the pieces 'Auntie' and 'marshmallows'. This image has been saved in the Auntie folder. Now reality differs from this image. Changes bother him, and he clearly demonstrates this.

The child has expectations in relation to the adult.

For example, when Dad takes Kim to bed, he always says: 'Nighty night, sleep tight'. When he once forgets, Kim cannot sleep. She recognizes the cohesion and handles it rigidly.

Grown-ups can meet the child's needs (halfway) on certain important points. It gives him a sense of security. Dad is predictable because he always says: 'Nighty night, sleep tight'. When a child gets a lot of clarity at home, and for example, people come to visit, at that moment persons change, and he may not be able to perform his usual duties. He gets upset, because the image does not fit anymore. This is why as a social worker I rarely visit people at home when the child is around, too.

8.6 'Sixth puzzle piece': Why

Being clear using 'The Essential 5' is at the core of guiding the autistic child. If it did not involve autistic children, the Why would naturally come in. But children with autism, failing to see the connections, do things from sheer habit, or because it is the thing to do, without worrying about underlying reasons. That is why the Why is not at the core of 'The Essential 5'. On one hand the child seems to take little interest in the underlying reason, or can even get angry or walk away when you explain things to him - because he does not understand what you are talking about.

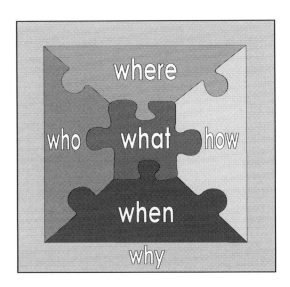

On the other hand, the child - especially if it is more intelligent - asks about the Why of things. This is why the Why belongs to 'The Essential 5', but merely as background information, which must be presented to the child matching his own particular needs.

After moving house, the whole family is busy unpacking and organising removal boxes. Tom (14) is sitting in a corner, quietly reading his comic book. He does not understand that he is expected to help out. Why should he... he feels like reading!

The Why-question is also a request for clarity. Why-questions from children with autism ask for auti-answers. An auti-answer is not an answer requiring understanding, such as:

(In a bus) 'Harry, stand up for that lady.' 'Why?' 'Because she's elderly.' 'So what?'

This may seem like a cheeky response coming from Harry, but he fails to see the connection between standing up and an elderly lady.
Neither is an auti-answer an answer involving emotion, such as:

'Could you please clear the table?' 'Why?' 'Because I am not feeling so well, you could help me a bit.' 'No, I won't!'

An auti-answer is an answer providing security and something to hold on to, because the factual answers are based on agreements and rules.
The Why-question may be asking for assurance and/or predictability, in which case the child wants to check if everything will go on just like before.

Why

auti-answer to
Why-question

62

'Why do I have to clear the table?' 'Because it is your turn', or: 'Because I say so. Because we have an agreement.' or: 'Because all children your age do that.'

'Why must I go to school?' 'In order to learn.' 'But I don't want to go to school.' 'All children go to school.' 'But I don't have to go to school every day, do I?' 'The government has decided that all children must go to school five days a week, and that means including you. All children do that until they are sixteen years old, so let's not talk about it anymore.'
Wonderful! No discussion, this will give him peace.

If you want the child to do something, give him an auti-answer after a Why-question and place the What directly in time by indicating What comes next.

'Why must I go to bed?' 'To sleep.' 'I don't want to.' 'You have to. In five minutes you pick up your bag, say goodnight and go upstairs.'

Mother wants Jasper to go away for a while, because she is talking to a social worker about him. Jasper asks: 'Why must I go to Auntie Carol?' 'Because we have agreed to do so. You will go play The Sims there. I will pick you up at 5 and then we will have pancakes for tea.'

Fred is totally upset, yelling from the computer he is using together with his sister. 'Why is it never my turn…? She always gets to go on the computer…!' Mother knows this is not true, but having put on her auti-specs, she ignores Fred's cries. Instead she addresses the two bickering children directively, thus applying structure: 'All right, we're making an agreement: you can each play for ten minutes, taking turns. When ten minutes are over, the other gets to play. Watch the clock. Fred can go now. At 4.30 it is Marianne's turn.'

auti-answer is based on facts, rules and agreements

auti-answer does not involve understanding and emotion

start

natural communication
as starting point

1

from natural communication
to auti-communication

heading for
auti-communication

2

9 Heading for auti-communication

A child with autism benefits from clarity and predictability, which can be achieved e.g. through 'The Essential 5.' But it is also important to adjust your own communication. Just like the child does everything differently, also the way he communicates is different. He just cannot help communicating the way he does - because he's different. This means you will have to learn to understand his way of communicating and adapt your own communication to his. In order to understand this special communication, we will first see how normal communication goes (i.e. without autism).

natural communication is communication without autism

9.1 Natural communication as starting point

Often we do not even realise how we communicate. We talk to one another without realising how conversation goes by. Still, in a smooth discussion there are several elements which make communication go smoothly and easily. Natural communication is called 'basic communication'. It means that there is interaction between people. For this, we use the following symbol:

This road sign stands for mutuality in basic communication. There is an exchange of information, which people convey through words, gestures, facial expressions, body language and tone of voice. When talking to each other, you observe your conversation partner. You pay attention to the other person's messages. You follow him, look at him and make eye contact. Your posture, your facial expressions and the way you are speaking are all friendly. You are inviting the other person to go on talking. When the other person is busy telling his story, you react by nodding or throwing in a few words. When your conversation partner finishes, you take over and react. All these elements are called the materials of natural basic communication. It is the way many people communicate: intuitively and naturally.

9.2 From natural communication to auti-communication
Natural communication consists of many elements. And exactly this causes a problem for the child with autism. Because of his limited understanding of both his own and the other person's inner self (TOM) and his incapability of having an overview of the entire situation, he has problems with most of the elements. He really is not capable of communicating the way we do. He does it in his own way. Differently, which does not mean: incorrectly.

Because the way we communicate is useless to him, we have to learn how to recognise his way of communication and adapt ourselves to this. Learning how to distinguish the characteristics (see below) means you can put on your 'auti-specs' and go along with the child's needs. This communication with the child is called auti-communication.

Auti-communication means one-way traffic. If you put your auti-specs on, you are able to recognise this.

This road sign stands for auti-communication. The child is incapable of adjusting to the way we communicate. He gets the white arrow, giving him right of way. We will have to adjust our communication (bottom arrow). By using auti-specs we can tune in to him. First and foremost you will have to get to understand the way he communicates, speaks and interprets our language.

We will explain this by means of three mind maps. The communication characteristics mentioned below are impeding the child to a lesser or greater degree because again this is different for each child.

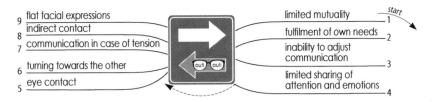

9 flat facial expressions
8 indirect contact
7 communication in case of tension
6 turning towards the other
5 eye contact

limited mutuality 1 start
fulfilment of own needs 2
inability to adjust communication 3
limited sharing of attention and emotions 4

10 Mind map 'Making contact'

The mind map 'Making contact' contains striking characteristics of the manner in which the autistic child makes contact with others.

10.1 Limited mutuality

limited mutuality

It attracts attention that a child with autism communicates starting from 'Me'. This is why in talks there is less mutuality. He mostly tells his own story instead of talking to you. This is because it is difficult for him to tune in to you. You are expecting too much from a child with autism, if you assume that he can be compassionate or think along with you like any other person. The rare occasions when he demonstrates this are considered a gift by parents.

Mum comes home from work, where she has learned that one of her colleagues is seriously ill. Miles (14) comes home from school and tells about the pebble he has found. Mum tells him about the illness of her immediate colleague, who visited them only last week. Miles just remarks: 'It is so smooth. And such a pretty colour...'

showing little interest

One of the striking aspects in children with autism is a limited interest in other people's perception of the environment. His impaired TOM causes the child to not understand the behaviour of the people around him, also making it impossible to predict. This is why it is difficult for him to catch on to people, to engage into or maintain friendships. In our communication with the child, we must take this into account. We cannot ask him to be quiet because his baby sister is sleeping, because he fails to tune in to the other person (Besides: what does 'quiet' mean here?). Performing a small task together, or playing a game, will only be successful if there is a certain level of mutuality or agreement, if not: it will go wrong.
How can we improve the process of these matters which advance with such difficulty? Give him a rule how to proceed in cases where things go wrong. You will have to supervise friendships longer, make more rules and make the other person predictable to the child.

You could say you are an interpreter between the child and his environment and vice versa. Let him tell his story first before you make contact with him. It is only after this that your words enter his mind.

10.2 Fulfilment of own needs

Most of the times, the child seeks contact with the other person in order to get things done he wants for himself: the fulfilment of his own needs is paramount. To him, the other is often merely an instrument. This is all the more conspicuous in children with lower intellectual powers. They can really grab your sleeve and drag you along to whatever it is they want, just like toddlers do. Autistic children who are more intelligent are better equipped to 'gift wrap' their wishes.

fulfilment of own needs is paramount

Jasper prefers to sit in his attic room in the dark, all day, on his computer. He does not come downstairs for a nice chat. He communicates only to find out things, to get an answer to his question, or to be helped. Najeeds case is less extreme: he makes contact and chats away nicely at first sight. Still, if you listen closely, it is almost exclusively his own story he wants to tell.

This belongs to children with autism. They cannot change it, which is something we must learn to accept.
If we want to get things done, for example reaching an agreement on when we are going to plan a common activity, we must plan for it in his schedule first. By no means every child is happy with the fact that we plan their schedules just like that. They want to be consulted and involved. The catch here is you starting a discussion (see explanation of Why? 8.6).

10.3 Inability to adjust communication

The child is unable to adjust his communication to others. He has his own way of telling a story and he can express himself only in one way. If you want to find out more about the way he thinks and about his motives, you will need to ask him more about details than about the big picture. For there may be another question hidden behind an announcement, question or recurrent phrase: the 'question behind the question'. Lack of perception of one own inner self's prevents that question from coming out. As a result, his environment often does not give him the desired answer, which may lead to a lot of frustration. Sometimes he does not even know that he has a question; often there is a hidden need of 'The Essential 5' behind the announcement.

inability to adjust communication

question behind the question

Alex (6) is playing in the living room after lunch. School has ended early today. He asks Mum: 'When are we going to have our meal?' Mother replies: 'We just had our lunch, didn't we?' Alex asks again: 'Yes, but when are we going to eat again?' 'Why, are you still hungry?' asks Mother. 'No,' says Alex. Mother does not understand.

Now we are putting on our auti-specs and look at the question behind the question: for Alex, does food have to do with feeling hungry? No, it is not that. Starting from what we know we now look at the things which are unclear to Alex.

Mother thinks: this afternoon off is just too long for him. He cannot command a view of it. His question should be interpreted as: What are the things I am going to do until we are having a meal again? If Mother divides this time into well-organized activities, Alex's' 'hunger issue' is solved.

Edward is playing on his play carpet which has roads on it. He asks where his old carpet has gone. Mother understands what question is behind this, and instead of merely replying: 'It is in the attic', she asks: 'Did you like that one better?' Now Edward can say, yes he did, because the old carpet's design and colours were not so loud.

Because he takes language literally and cannot adjust it to the situation, it may well be that he does not understand someone else's words.

At school, Martin is in the circle. The teacher says: 'We are done now. Put your chair back behind your table.' This seems to be straight forward, but while all the other children are back at their tables, Martin is still sitting in the circle. He has failed to understand that 'we' includes him as well. Martin still needs to be addressed personally as well.

For children with autism it is incomprehensible that it is OK to say something in one situation which you are not allowed to say in another situation.

At home, the family refers to the neighbours as 'the fat' and 'the skinny' neighbour. Laura (19) uses this term to address one of the neighbours directly: 'Hey fat neighbour, look, I've got an ice cream.'

We will have to adjust our communication to that of the child, because the other way round is just impossible. We cannot expect Laura to understand that this is not the thing to say to your neighbour. There are three things we can do:

1) Close off the word 'fat' - which she uses for this neighbour - and replace it with another word;
2) Inform the neighbour and leave it at that;
3) Give Laura a rule: at home we say 'fat neighbour' and when you see him, you call him John.

10.4 Limited sharing of attention and emotions

In children with autism it catches the eye at an early age already that it is difficult for him to share something, when both children are drawn to it. This makes enjoying something together scarce. In this case especially, it is important for the environment to continue naming his enjoyment and enjoying this unique child, never ceasing to share attention with him. In other words: holding on to the natural basic contact in an adjusted manner.

'Look, John. Mum is wearing new shoes. Aren't they lovely?'
John (8), special primary education, glances over the shoes briefly and turns to his book again.

With this brief phrase, Mother has had some shared attention from John. She does not expect him to compliment her on her new shoes, because he has not yet learned how to do that. Still, it is in John's best interest to have his attention drawn to (changes in) his environment. Mother can teach John how to say something nice, as a courtesy (see Chapter 21).

10.5 Eye contact

For many autistic children it is difficult to make plenty of eye contact during a conversation. Instead, they make eye contact briefly and quickly: also called 'fleeting eye contact'.
I sometimes hear: 'He makes eye contact very well, so he cannot have an autistic disorder'. This is untrue. Making eye contact can be acquired. Besides, not all people with some form of autism have trouble looking someone else in the eye. It is true, however, that the information coming from the other person's eyes means little to a child with autism. So make less eye contact yourself, especially if you feel it is bothering him. It is possible that he may get too many surplus stimuli which may inhibit his functioning.

limited sharing of attention

fleeting eye contact

10.6 Turning towards the other

not turning towards the other

Some children with autism turn their backs on you and just babble. It turns out that this is meant for you. They have not yet learned to turn to someone but just 'launch' their words into space. It is possible that they have not yet discovered the other as a means to achieve their goals. It may also be that they find it hard to look someone in the eye. Also, it is possible that they have not yet discovered language as a means of communication.

Tim (6) does not talk, but every now and then you hear a word coming from his mouth. Until Mother discovers that when she is singing, Tim is trying to repeat the last word. She starts practising with Tim. Initially, she sings slowly and repeats the same words over and over again. This triggers Tim's speech.
Tim's mother fits in very well with whatever initiatives Tim demonstrates. Mother goes on practising by continuing to sing. Apart from this, pre-verbal speech therapy is started up. Now Tim never ceases talking. The singing practice teaches Tim where the voice comes from. He pays more and more attention to Mother's mouth. At first he was turning away when Mother was talking, now he turns to her whenever she starts to talk.

We will have to be on the look-out for the fact that a child with autism is talking to us, although he is turning away. We have to keep in mind as well that he can hear what we are saying, even though he is not looking.

10.7 Communication in case of tension

communication more difficult in case of tension

When the child gets more tense, communication deteriorates. This tension indicates: 'Give me clarity in the here and now. Give me a hold on my life by predicting what is going to happen next. And: give me 5 pieces.' When the child is edgy, it is best to keep your sentences as brief as possible. Friendly orders help him more than explaining what he should and should not be doing. Just tell him friendly but firmly what it is that you want: him to do and give him clarity using 'The Essential 5'. This can also be described as leading back to the What. There is a clear task, taking away the tension from the child.
Point out visible things in order to distract him. Stop him when he is talking too much, because this is only confusing him. In case of tension, it is best to ignore negative behaviour. It is better to provide the child with something to do.

10.8 Indirect contact

Sometimes it is easier for the child to communicate through an object (hand doll, cuddly toy, note, drawing, telephone). To him it this is sometimes easier than having to look someone in the eye. You can use this when communicating with him. Especially if important educational moments are involved, the advantage being that less eye contact is required. This makes it easier to hold on to the basic idea, because using pen and paper prompts your memory. Drawings may be used to support the child's visual thinking.

After school, Vicky's mother uses a hand doll in order to talk over the school day. Without doll, Mother does not get Vicky to talk. The doll is a means which helps her tell her stories.

10.9 Flat facial expressions

Many children with autism have flat facial expressions. Because they cannot understand the other's animated facial expressions, it will be very difficult for them to acquire these themselves.

You can improve his skills by watching photographs together showing a variety of facial expressions. By analysing and linking words to those expressions, the child sees more and more that faces can demonstrate the same emotion (for example angry, happy or sad), even if the details vary. By taking pictures of his own 'funny faces' you can also teach him to see what his own face is capable of.

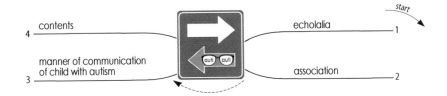

4 — contents

echolalia — 1

manner of communication
of child with autism

association — 2

3 —

11 Mind map 'Talk'
The mind map Talk contains characteristics of the speech of a child with autism which may attract attention.

11.1 Echolalia (parroting)
A child with autism excels in remembering something which the other says, and use it again in another place, at another time. Sometimes this is appropriate, sometimes it is not. But it is always a trap to his environment. It turns out that he has not learned to master the words he is using. So check, by means of asking questions, reiterating his answers as questions and persisting, if he really understands what he is saying.

echolalia

'You say you find your teacher terribly creative. So, what does she do to make you think so?' 'Every day I come to school, my teacher has already arrived,' replies Marie. Marie has heard that her teacher is creative, but she does not know what the word means. If I had not persisted, I would think that Marie uses the word creative correctly, and that her teacher is creative.

11.2 1 - 1 association
A one-to-one association is an absolute link the child creates using various puzzle pieces. For example, a link between a person and an object, between a task and a fixed place, or a task and a fixed time. But words or certain situations and persons can be connected, too: it is all possible. The connection is absolute and the child often implements it rigidly. To us, such a link often looks odd.

making absolute
connections

In communication, the child may also permanently relate different matters to each other.

Peter has two teachers; one of them wears her hair in a ponytail. Peter has made the connection between teacher and ponytail, and says: 'Miss Ponytail is coming today.' He has given her this name. He knows her real name, but when mentioning her, it is always 'Miss Ponytail' (detailed observation).

One of the guest house's counsellors enters the living room,
where Brian and Sam are doing something which is not allowed.
Sam sees her and yells to Brian, who has PPD-NOS: 'She's
coming!' Months later he stills calls her 'she's coming'.

1 - 1 association

1 - 1 associations are saved in a brain folder. It is possible to
close off this folder, but only if you replaced it by a new one.

Whenever Gareth (24) sees a woman with a big bra size, he
says out loud: 'I see two big boobs!' Gareth is told what he can
do: put his hands over his mouth and then say: 'I see two big
boobs.'

11.3 How to communicate with a child with autism
The voice of a child with autism may sound monotonous
because he cannot understand what intonation means. It is
difficult for him to imitate or adopt this from others as well. Apart
from this, it may be that his manner of speech sounds grown-
up, or pedantic as a teacher might sound. All of this has to do
with his limited possibilities of fine-tuning to his environment and
peers. He does not know How to do that.
One of my father's poem reflects very well how he is struggling
with the way we communicate (but the way he expresses this,
as in this poem, remains very special....) In a group conversation or school circle conversation a child with autism will have
trouble keeping track of the others. The other opinions are all
mixed up and the child observes them as odd, independent
jigsaw puzzle pieces. If you want to debate something, you must
be able to see the big picture and to compare components.
Being capable of abstract thinking is often required, too. Autistic
children usually go without these skills. As a rule they will attract
your attention because in such a discussion they put the wrong
puzzle pieces together.

how to....

Language

Here and there my language
may sound pompous
but that, that is something
I can be excellent in
Almost without thinking
the words I am exploiting
Modern or antique:
an entire language clique

I am lofty,
a little bit insipid,
behaving snobbily
and pretty out of date.

Rational associations
in regular conversations,
that is is how I've
often taken a nose-dive.

They can hear me skip
from one thing to another
and don't know that inside
I am linking without a bother
So, I fail to see connecting themes
in every conversation
I am irrelevant
a nuisance to others.

One also sees that the child is not taking part in the discussion. The discussion which the child brings up himself, can be a means to get a 100% clarity about how things will proceed. It is him asking questions and you answering, actually. Next he pursues a detail of your answer, making you think something does not fit. Next, a discussion arises, whereas all the child wanted to do was ask a question to get more clarity. This clarity required by the child can be pictured as a 'square task'. When in this square form anything - even the tiniest detail - is unclear to the child, it gets upset or confused and gives up. It is quite possible for a verbally strong child to enter a discussion about the 'opening'. It is your challenge to recognize this 'hole' and understand that it is merely a question from the child to get absolute clarity.

avoiding
discussion

74

Therefore don't be tempted to start a discussion, because for him this will only add to the indistinctness. You can help the child by closing the hole for him. This you can do by explaining to him - at detail level - what is going on and make distinct agreements if necessary.

While preparing to go to school in the morning, Rachael finds her tyre punctured. Because of her autism she thinks along straight lines. No bike, no school. Her mother disagrees. A discussion arises about the importance of going to school. (This involves understanding and Rachael cannot follow. To her, her future does not have anything to do with a punctured tyre). During the discussion Mother indicates that she can take the bus. It is true she may be a little late, but it is better than not going at all. Mother observes the uncertainty in Rachael's eyes who nearly gets into a panic because of this unexpected event. By starting a discussion, Mother expects Rachael to go but it is all in vain. The change from bike to bus makes things so unclear that she cannot cope with it spontaneously. She has questions such as: 'How is it that bus tickets work again?' and 'What should I say when I enter the class room too late?' Although Rachael is a very self-supporting girl who normally can solve this kind of problems all by herself, these unexpected changes make her 'freeze'. All she wants to do is stay at home. Mother knows that once this routine has been introduced, it will quickly become a rule to her autistic child.

seeking discussion is a request for clarity, too

What Rachael needs, is for Mother to take control and make a decision about the How and the What, now that the situation has changed. Mother can do this by saying: 'I'll get my keys, I will take you to school in the car and you will be on time. After school you will repair your puncture. And tomorrow you can go to school by bike again.' Thus, Mother avoids a discussion, is clear about the What and gives structure to How things will go. Also, she indicates that this situation is an exception to the rule and everything will be normal again tomorrow.

I will make your lunch

Still, Rachael finds the very last teeny hole which she needs to be fixed (snippet of uncertainty), saying: 'But my lunch for school isn't ready yet!' Mother closes this last little hole by saying: 'Put on your coat and get your bag. I will make your lunch and off we go.' Only now everything is clear to Rachael, her panic ebbing away. She can be at peace now.

11.4 Contents

The contents of whatever it is a child with autism is saying, is a direct result of his thinking. In Chapter 2, I have already explained that, because of his jigsaw puzzle observation, his thinking works out differently as well. The puzzle in his head is just as crooked as the words he utters. He uses the pieces from another puzzle which causes him to make wrong connections. Some children's sentences are not fluent yet, you could say they are stammering. They glue together the wrong pieces, resulting in a lack of logic. Carl gets lost and remarks: 'I have lost my way.'

Mum is crying. Vincent sees this and Mum explains it is because she has a heart ache. 'Mum, I know why you are not feeling well. The doctor tells you to eat this special food (cholesterol lowering). Today you had chips, that's why your heart is aching now.'

Vincent does not understand that eating chips once does not cause heart problems. Besides, he fails to notice that Mum's heart ache has to do with personal relationships. What are the consequences of this for his communication? Because of his limited understanding of the other person, he can come across as self-centred. This, however, is a result of his disorder which he cannot help. Neither can you. The only thing is to accept him just like he is and hand him instruments to make him more skilful socially (also see Chapters 21 through 23).

Because of his limited TOM the child has little perception of what he wants, likes or needs himself. His environment must be extra attentive to this. For how can a child ask for help if he does not even know that he is unable to do something or needs something?

what he is saying

Andy (3) is taking a shower, turning the knob. He makes the water run as hot as possible and just stands there. At one point, his mother comes to take a look and sees he looks as red as a lobster. Andy does not know what he needs, therefore cannot ask for help, phrase his pain or act by himself.

Restricted knowledge of his inner self makes it sometimes hard for the child to answer questions like: 'How are you feeling?' 'What do you want?' 'Will you join us?' 'What do you think of this?' 'What do you feel like?' If you notice that he has trouble with this, you can help him by providing 'subtitles' indicating his possible wishes: 'You are not feeling well because you have a cold', 'I think you'd like sweets rather than a biscuit', 'You will join in the football game. You love that! I know that, because you are fond of football.' Or: 'We will go on a bike trip this afternoon, that will be fun.'

How...?
What...?
Why...?

If you approach him like this, in a definite manner, it is easier for him to respond to what it is he wants or does not want. This approach, however, should not be aimed at imposing your will on him, but on making it easier for him to know what he wants.

When shaking someone else's hand, Josh (21) gives everybody a sound slap on the shoulder. He has seen someone do that once. From that moment on, he has picked up this habit, without being able to assess if a person welcomes it, or is bothered by it. The slap on the shoulder is rather harsh on ladies. Josh is 6 ft 5, and rather strong. Josh needs a rule about Who he can slap on the shoulder, and How he should greet other people.

using body language

Because the child has little consideration for others, conflicts often arise. Especially between siblings. For example, it is always he who should have the remote control. Or he gets hold of the common bowl of crisps and finishes it virtually by himself.
Of his own accord, it is very difficult for the child with autism to be considerate of others, to be able to share. He must be trained for each and every situation, by means of 'The Essential 5'.
When talking to him, it is important to keep in mind that he cannot always see logical connections, which is a result of his defective view of connections. The consequences for communication can be big. The wrong puzzle pieces are put together. Linguistic usage can demonstrate this, the sentences not coming out fluently but stumbling.

My son used to give me notes saying: 'Mum I love you, from Mum from George.' He talks like this sometimes, too. Also parts of sentences or compound words get switched round sometimes.

'When I am in my bed, I sleep afall.' Carl uses this combination a lot, because he has linked the words together like this. Carl also uses a 'flannel face' and waits for the 'light traffics' to turn green. At Easter time, he draws 'bunny easters.'

When phrasing events it often happens that Carl gets hold of the wrong puzzle pieces, which means his story is not in accordance with the actual facts.

i sleep afall

Thus, Carl is prone to be accused of lying. The opposite is true, for children with autism hardly ever lie. Because it requires quite a lot of TOM. You must be able to predict what the other is thinking and how he will react, and how you can benefit, if you are lying. For a child with autism this is usually far too complex so he cannot see the connections.

Carl's truth is a result of the way he makes connections and his perception of the big picture's coherence. It is useless to try and enter a discussion about this, for you cannot convince him that you are right. He has made his puzzle, and he is unable to think along your lines.

The story of an autistic child can come across as chaotic. You can't make head or tail of it, with excessive details. Help him hold on to the basic idea.

Some children must not be interrupted, however. They lose track of their story and must start all over again. This may require a lot of patience.

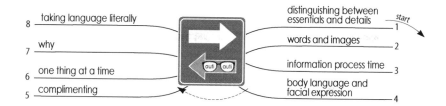

8   taking language literally

7   why

6   one thing at a time

5   complimenting

distinguishing between essentials and details   *start* 1

words and images 2

information process time 3

body language and facial expression 4

12 Mind map 'Understanding communication'

The mind map 'Understanding communication' explains how the child's perception of another person's communication works, and how you can handle this.

12.1 Distinguishing between essentials and details
It is difficult for the child to distinguish between essentials and details when there is one big mess of words. This makes it very important to communicate with him in brief, concise sentences, being expressly definite (without any doubt) and using understandable language. If the child does not understand what you are saying: check if the information you have given him was complete. If you want to let him know you understand him: affirm this by literally repeating what he has said.
Being brief, concise and definite and supplying full information is done by means of 'The Essential 5'. Next, be clear and predictable. This does not mean that you can't be nice and friendly. On the contrary, the child also needs to hear and feel that you care about him, and appreciate him for what he is. Demonstrate this in an appropriate manner (adapted to him). Use a 'business-like' approach to allow information to get into his head well. Cling to the basic idea of the conversation yourself.
Many children with autism have trouble relating something in a brief and terse manner. A lot of irrelevant things occur to them in the process.

Ryan wants to tell about his day at school. 'Do you really want to know everything?' 'Yes, go ahead.' He cannot be stopped and tells about his day down to the last detail. It is difficult for Ryan to distinguish between essentials and details; every detail matters to him.

all information matters

12.2 Words and images

Words are volatile. They are gone as soon as you have uttered them. It is more difficult for him to cling to words in his head and make them re-appear than to remember images of something he has seen. Take advantage of this by visualizing with him or on his behalf (see starting from Chapter 17).

12.3 Information process time

He needs to put the puzzle pieces together and give meaning to them before he can understand something and react to it. In communication, this means his reaction usually comes a little later (time to think = time to puzzle). Reaction time may vary between a few seconds and even a couple of weeks. For a grown-up it then becomes almost incomprehensible what he is talking about. Because of the extra puzzle time required he is usually a little slower at making handicrafts, understanding how something works, or performing an order.

Grown-ups want children to do things right now. Give this child time to puzzle and time to implement the order into his own programme.

12.4 Body language and facial expressions

The child hardly understands the other person's body language or facial expressions. This is because everybody looks different, when you look at the details of facial expressions. This does not provide enough grip. 'Are you angry?' is a question which Luke asks a lot. He does not see it, which is why he is asking. We can help the child by giving a name to our emotions – even if he is not asking for an explanation – and phrasing what we would otherwise be expressing through body language. This is what I sometimes call 'subtitling'.

He is sad because he does not have no work he has no friends either from school becos he is different than others but he wants to be treated just like others this al belons to autism

12.5 Complimenting

It is of vital importance for the child with autism to receive positive affirmation from his environment. Compliments wrapped in language, however, do not come across. The What being successful often pleases him more than a sincere compliment. Therefore link compliments to concrete facts or tasks so he will better understand what the compliment is for.

linking compliments to tasks or facts

Martin catches the ball, Mother says: 'Well done!' Martin is hearing and seeing all kinds of things, which causes him to not understand if Mother is referring to catching the ball. Is she talking about the birds singing maybe or that car just passing by? Mother's compliment does come across when she says: 'You did very well catching that ball!'

12.6 One thing at a time

The child can do only one thing at a time. If he is required to give an answer to something, for example, he stops doing what he was doing for a brief moment. Therefore, it is best to give simple orders which are linked to actions.

For a lot of children it is true as well that when they are eating, they are eating. Not much can be added. Being touched by the person next to him or questions asked tend to yield frustration. When the child is just telling something himself, being interrupted bothers him a lot. He must be able to finish his story. Sometimes, after an interruption, he has to start all over again because that is how the puzzle image is stored in his head, and not half of it.

one step at a time

The child has trouble making choices. This is because he cannot form a picture of possible consequences because of his limited ability to see their cohesion. You can help him by making a selection beforehand. Offer him what is in store: 'Would you like orange soda or coke?' instead of asking: 'Would you like a drink?'

You help him by offering him a limited number of options. The same goes for deliberations. Here, too, the child is incapable of considering options and consequences. Do not discuss more information than he can deal with. Keep more complex considerations to yourself and let him know the outcome as an accomplished fact.

Jake has to switch schools: from his neighbourhood school to a special education school. His parents have three options. When they discuss these options with Jake, he gets totally upset, because he is unable to have a view of the consequences of the various choices (limited CC and TOM). It goes better when Jake's parents make a choice and inform him of the outcome: which school it is, when he will start, which teacher he will have and when he can go and have his first look around.

12.7 Why

Today, a lot of things are explained to children. People elaborate on the 'Why' of things. Pros and cons are discussed with children. Choices are being substantiated. But how to deal with this kind of thing when a child with autism is involved? It makes you so much more clear when you don't do this. The child cannot handle a large number of words: he gets 'flooded'. Apart from this, he cannot keep up with your insight in the pros and cons, because he lacks view and perception himself.

Why

Therefore he asks for a different kind of distinctness which boils down to: 'Give me facts, rules or agreements, so I know where I stand.' What made you decide so usually leaves him indifferent. Children who are more intelligent ask about the Why themselves most of the time. They, too, do not require explanations involving understanding or emotion but explanations phrased as facts based on rules and agreements.

On the other hand, your story may trigger a discussion. They keep saying 'Yes, but...', which is a result of their associative thinking. When you notice the child getting confused, offer clarity by stopping his thinking. Cut short the 'Yes, but...', or meet each argument with a fact. Facts give much-needed clarity.

Max (14, PDD-NOS) is at the table with his parents and brother Tim. Both children's cell phones are next to their plates. Tim taps a bit on his. Max receives a text message. He exclaims, full of astonishment: 'How does O2 know I am making so much noise when I am eating?'
Max does not understand that it was Tim who sent him the text message.

Because of their limited TOM this goes for feelings, too. A child with autism cannot put himself in your shoes, meaning that your feelings do not motivate him to do what you are asking: 'I am not feeling so well… can you please set the table for me?' The answer will be 'no' most of the time. Because he has a limited perception of your feelings, it is (almost) impossible for him to take them into consideration. Your emotions do not motivate him to help you. So how can you make him do something you expect him to do? The child will understand you better when you are in keeping with his logical way of arguing. When you offer him facts and rules, the Why becomes clear to him; it matches the way his mind works. 'I am sick (is a fact) and you will set the table at 5 o' clock (the What).'

you must be able to see the cohesion in order to understand 'Why'

He may offer resistance because this involves a change. In this case: don't start a discussion and be adamant. (Which can be tough when you are ill). In the end he will do it. The more often you stand firm, the easier it is for him to perform these orders, provided you give him some process time.

When he does something which really makes you angry, do not demonstrate your anger. If you do this, you as a person will change. He can get totally upset: the safe person which gave him something to hold on to, is gone. This may result in panic. If you want him to stop doing something from then on, give him a rule about how to proceed next time.

I had been angry with my child for years, when I finally figured out how things work. Every time he got so upset that for weeks on end I received daily notes saying 'I love you.' Every time he was thinking I did not love him anymore, his notes being a question: 'Do you still love me?' Then I told him (we made an agreement) that I will always love him. Always meaning: now and tomorrow and in ten years' time and even when I am dead. Always means when he has left home, is angry with me or is doing something he is not allowed to, too. I put this in writing and we made the agreement that from then on, I would tell him whenever I am angry, that I will tell him why and explain what it is he should do, and I will not get cross anymore.

From that moment on, there are no more notes saying 'I love you.' A pity really, but also a sign that we understand each other better again.

12.8 Taking language literally
The child takes language literally.

*Whenever James goes to the toilet, he pees on the toilet rim.
His mother grumbles about this, but also tells James what he
should do, which is: urinating while seated. James has the habit
of never closing the door when going to the toilet. This is the
reason why Mother had the opportunity to take a peek when
he went for a pee a few days later. To her great astonishment
she finds James sitting on the floor, trying to pee in the toilet
from there. She cries out in amazement: 'James, what are you
DOING?' 'Peeing while sitting,' James tells her, 'you told me so,
didn't you?'*

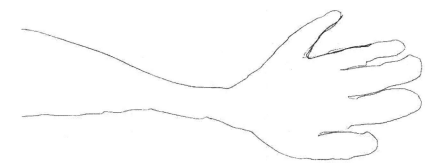

Therefore, your linguistic usage must be concrete and
unambiguous.The child fails to understand puns or ambiguous
remarks because he cannot see the hidden meaning. Sarcastic
remarks can completely upset him.

*'You are such a sweet little thing,' someone tells Annie.
She replies: 'You cannot eat me, can you?'*

*'Hey pretty face!' somebody calls Meg, who reacts in
amazement: 'I have a body, too!'*

don't use:
don't touch
stop doing

For autistic children, orders which are stated negatively are
often difficult to manage, too. In order to understand he must
have imagination and be able to see the connections as in: if I
do not do this, she expects me to do that. Because of the lack
of imagination and perception of connections it is better to
literally tell him what he should do, instead of saying what he
cannot do. This will often be hard to think of, but it is certainly
worth the trouble, because it will make the child listen to you.
Usually it is difficult for a child with autism to give a meaning to
words like 'later', 'maybe' 'in a minute' 'don't know yet' or 'a
little while'. Avoid these as much as possible and be concrete
about your points, with a view to time as well as the What.

This also goes for questions like: 'Would you please set the table?' He does not feel like it, so he says 'No.' If it is not a question to you, do not make a question of it but just announce it. Only then you will be clear.

'I'm Eric. And who are you?' the new teacher asks Sebastian. 'I'm not,' replies Sebastian.

Somebody is waving friendly at John, who reacts as follows: 'Don't hit me!'

Mary-Ann does not want to go to school because she is ill. Mother does not notice anything unusual about her. Mary-Ann is absolutely certain that she is ill because her teacher said so yesterday: Miss said: 'You're feeling hot, I think you are about to fall ill.'

Emily (lower secondary professional education) is dancing in the school yard. Not because she likes dancing so much, but because her class mates told her to. They stand by and watch, jeering at her.

During a break, the teacher tells Fred: 'Stop playing football here.' Fred picks up the ball and starts kicking it again some ten yards away. The teacher was referring to 'in the school yard' while Fred is thinking 'Not right here', so he finds himself a new spot somewhere in the school yard.

Can't play football here? Alright.

One minute later, ten yards farther on

Teacher to Chris: 'Yes of course, that's right, scribble away!' Which is something Chris readily complies with.

Carl burps out loud in the class room. The teacher reacts by saying: 'If you dare do that again...' to which Carl immediately reacts by burping again. The teacher gets angry with Carl, who is really oblivious of any guilt: 'Master told me to burp again, didn't he?'

be concrete! say what you really mean!

When managing children with autism, it is very important to realise What we are saying and How. One thing we should not do is blame them for our own blurred communication.

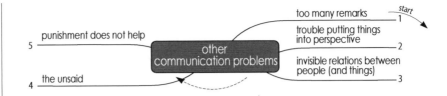

	too many remarks	start 1
5 — punishment does not help	other communication problems	trouble putting things into perspective 2
4 — the unsaid		invisible relations between people (and things) 3

13 Other communication problems

13.1 Too many remarks

the child never stops talking...

When everybody is getting tired of the child's comments, it is the grown-up's duty to take over control and stop the child in a very decisive manner. The child is bothered, too, by his not being able to stop. His head turns into a chaos, and all he gets is negative criticism.

Eric claims every person he encounters. He starts talking without considering the fact if the other wants to listen at all. Thus, he goes on and on about his adventures. For decency's sake, you cannot just walk away from him, which is why people are starting to avoid Eric.

You can stop him by agreeing upon a clear 'stop'. This is a key word which can be used in every situation (see Chapter 18 about how to deal with this).

13.2 Having trouble to put things into perspective

teaching him to put things into perspective by providing standard sentences

Because the child cannot see the connection (the link), he is incapable of classifying and placing information. This is why he gets swamped by stimuli. It is impossible for him to look at it from a distance and think, for example: 'Well, it is not so bad, is it?' Or: 'Never mind, it will soon be over' (putting things into perspective).

Lorraine is bothered a lot by external stimuli swamping here. A fly landing on her hand means a stimulus she cannot ignore. She stops doing whatever it was she was doing. All she can do, is react to the fly. Whenever she goes to a care farm, the flies severely disrupt her daily activities.

The flies can be managed if they are being put into perspective. This is done by giving her a standard sentence: 'Flies belong to a farm'. After some practise she has created a new mind folder about how life at the farm should look like: including the flies. Because she can now place it, she is capable of ignoring the stimulus and continue. She can stop the stimulus by herself now. When a fly is bothering her in some other location, she uses this sentence as well and can go on with her activity.

13.3 Invisible relationships between people (and things)

People have relationships: emotional ties, unwritten mutual agreements and so on. All of this is invisible to the eye and therefore hardly concrete to someone with autism. He does not sense it, which sometimes results in his hurting others unintentionally or makes a fool of himself without noticing himself. What behaviour should be shown to which people is even more difficult. Who do you kiss, who don't you kiss, and how often?

what he cannot
see, isn't there

George comes home with a black eye. In the pub he has made the mistake of telling another boy that he thinks the girl next to him is cute and that he would like to go steady with her. He has not been able to conclude from the couple's behaviour that they are having a relationship.

By providing him with rules on paper, the child can be taught to demonstrate proper behaviour (see Chapter 21, about how you can teach him this using the behaviour contract).

13.4 The unsaid

Children with autism have difficulty with the unsaid as well. As opposed to children without autism, who are capable of understanding the other person.

what he cannot
hear, hasn't
happened

Mother is crying because Grandpa died. John (12) reacts by saying: 'It is 5.30. I want my tea now.'

Things will improve once you clarify – by naming each detail – what an incident like this means to you and how you are feeling. It is important to label your body language and facial expressions, too. Phrase his grief as well, and tell him how to demonstrate his sorrow. This is how he will learn to phrase his emotions. In particular, make concrete what is going to change from now on. For example: we won't be visiting Grandpa on Wednesdays anymore. Give him an alternative: from now on we will go into town on Wednesday.

Mariella holds her own at the training centre she attends, by imitating the linguistic usage of the other children.
She addresses her teacher in these terms, too. She is sent from the class room regularly because of her big mouth. That is not what she intends, of course. How should Mariella know that speaking to the teacher and speaking to a class mate are two different things, if nobody tells her? Mariella has yet to learn what she can say to whom.

13.5 Punishment does not work

The punishing adult wants the child to learn that his behaviour is uncalled-for and that he should not do that anymore.

But punishment does not or hardly work for a child with autism. Because understanding is required from the child to link the punishment to the behaviour. Even if he would be able to do so, it would still be almost impossible to imagine what the desirable behaviour should be like. The latter is too complex for a majority of autistic children.

Most parents of children with autism find out soon enough. But the environment may react in amazement when it is observed that parents do not punish their children, especially when the child demonstrates quite a lot of negative or obnoxious behaviour. One may hear pedantic remarks like: 'You should be harder on him' or 'Let him stay with me for a week..'.

People making this kind of remarks have little understanding of the problems the child has to face day by day, and hardly take the parents seriously.

The child often links a reward to a certain activity. He expects the same reward the next time instead of demonstrating proper behaviour again. Omitting the reward can result in a loss of the appropriate behaviour. The only thing to do is: tell him what he should do and visualising this if possible.

punishment teaches him nothing tell him what it is he should do

14 Using auti-communication

In communicating with a child with autism it is a must to fit in with his way of observing, thinking and communicating. Including your knowledge and understanding of this unique child it is possible to have a successful contact. You can acquire auti-communication as explained in the previous chapters. Below is a summary of points of attention which you can consider when talking to a child with autism.

Auti-communication hints
- Be clear and predictable in your communication.
- Keep up with his story first, only then he will be able to keep up with you.
- Observe and follow your child through auti-specs.
- He rather has an order than a question.
- Let your attitude and communication be friendly but resolute.
- Label the things you want in an emphatic, decisive, concrete and detailed manner - using 'The Essential 5'.
- Let there be no doubt in the way you talk and act.
- 'Subtitle' your own and his behaviour, emotions, sensory experiences, thoughts and the situation to be expected.
- Avoid 'Why'-questions.

- When he is being a pest, he is doing a test, i.e. looking for clarity. So be clearer!
- Adjust your cracks or avoid them. Do not use sarcasm.
- Help him hold on to the basic idea.
- Do not enter into a discussion.
- Keep your own emotions under control.
- Explain the Why of something on the basis of facts, rules and agreements, not on the basis of understanding or emotion.
- Let your body language and linguistic usage be unambiguous.
- In your contact with him, consider his sensory hypersensitivity.
- Be friendly in posture as well as in facial expression and intonation.
- Do not convert your own impotence into anger aimed at the child but into a task (the What).
- If there are things still 'under consideration', do not share them with your child.
- If you cannot give him clarity right now, indicate when it will be clear.
- Do not take it personally if he makes insulting remarks.
- Allow for time to think for the processing of information.
- If he lingers and gets stuck, close his mind map.
- Provide visual support if he does not do as told.
- Look for the 'question behind the question.'
- Meet agreements and promises meticulously. Stick to the agreed time.

start

person-dependent 1

2 structure-dependent

teaching the child

15 Teaching the child

Experience has taught me that a lot of children could develop further if they were offered the right structure. If you have knowledge of the autistic disorder you can put on your auti-specs, recognize the behaviour and see that it is a result of the disorder. This makes it easier to think up what the child needs in order to understand and pick up the What. You know how he communicates and how you can tune in to him. The starting point always is: being clear and predictable. Which is what you are when you are using 'The Essential 5' and applying auti-communication.

Of course a lot of things go well, too, and there is plenty of behaviour which does not need to be fixed. All is well that goes well. Do not apply unnecessary structure. The things that do go wrong, however - this may involve seemingly simple things - must be taught to the child, for only then will he develop.

This can be done on the basis of rules or step-by-step plans. We expect the child to do something of his own accord in the end, as long as you tell him or show him often enough. But this is by no means always the case in children with autism. This is caused by a lack of understanding of the coherence. Therefore, the introduction of coherence is the answer to his question. Visualise subsequent steps, so he can actually see the coherence. By going through these steps over and over again, using visual aids, the cohesion grinds down in his brain and he will pick it up. When the child has become self-reliant in performing a task, the visual aids can be omitted in the long run. Below is the description of an approach for the guidance of a child with autism towards as much self-support as possible.

15.1 Person-dependent

Babies are totally dependent on their parents or attendants. Normally speaking the child develops and becomes more and more self-supporting. When a child with autism remains dependent of the grown-up and takes his sense of security from that as well, it is very vulnerable. When the other is lost or changes, the child - who is so devoted to constancy - has a problem. This is a very strenuous situation for the adult. It takes a lot of effort to support every single (subsequent) action. Just as it is tiring to always have to be clear and predictable.

person-dependent

By nature, children with autism are not easily inclined to break away from the parent. The parent will have to start off this release process consciously, which is rather unnatural. As a matter of fact, the grown-up should try to make himself or herself as redundant as possible. By handing the child certain tools (such as teaching him to take a shower at a fixed time, so the parent does not have to say that anymore), the person-dependability disappears more or less.

give the child space by breaking away from him

It is in the best interest of the child growing up that the parents have to make choices to slowly withdraw from situations in which, with a view to the child's age, supervision is no longer appropriate. As the child does still need supervision, a visual structure can take over that role.

15.2 Structure-dependent

Dependability on a visualised order is much more predictable and much clearer than person-dependability. Everything happens at a fixed time, in a fixed place, with fixed persons, in a fixed manner. The child is dependent on that structure because otherwise he is not (yet) capable to perform tasks on his own. We aim at the environment applying this structure for the child, but only where needed (do not apply structure just for structure's sake). On the contrary, it is all about the structure becoming an aid on the way to more self-support. Possibly the child will be able to operate independently in the future, without this aid.

structure-dependent

John, turning a page of his icons folder (see Chapter 16), sees a picture of a sock. He puts on his sock. After that, the same goes for the other sock. John turns another page and sees his briefs. So he puts on his briefs.

In children with autism who are able to perform tasks independently, with or without the help of visual aids, this will always be a 'conditional independence'.

Brian goes to the supermarket every day. One day the pavement is digged up. This makes the way to the supermarket no longer identifiable to Brian. He turns around and goes home without his purchases. It is quite possible for Brian to go shopping on his own. But he needs the presence of details important to him, otherwise he will panic.

When a child has reached the stage in which he can perform tasks on his own, you often see him handling changes in a far more flexible manner. It is exactly because he has acquired the ordinary course of events that he has something to go by when changes occur.

You can prepare the child for sudden changes. When supervised, it is possible to make the change predictable, too.

At Geraldine's home Wednesday is 'chips day'. But Mother has run out of chips. So she says: 'There will be no chips today but macaroni, because we're out of chips. Next Wednesday we will eat chips again.' This enables Geraldine to cope with the change. The task (the What = eating chips) is 'put intotime' (next Wednesday). This is a form of saying When it will happen. 'Putting into time' is very helpful to the child. The What is planned, so it is OK.

At first, the task which is performed self-supportingly will be restricted to a particular location or time. Gradually the child will be able to make generalizations with regard to other places and other situations. When laid out in a framework, this development looks as follows:

Development framework of the autistic child

| Child's growth | | | | | person-dependent | | structure-dependent | self-supporting |

		person-dependent		structure-dependent	self-supporting
Grown-up's action	**TASK**	acquiring task	check yourself	visualise	persist	supervision
	HOW	Everything = task - skills - communication - socially	(auti) (auti) auti-specs on? - clear and predictable? - auti-communication?	made-to-measure subsequent actions, visualising	teach how to perform tasks by practice and consistent control	- under conditions - learning how to generalise

15.3 On his own
The child with autism does not take action of his own accord to develop most of the time and stays dependent on grown-up persons. In order to help him grow it is the grown-up who must take action. When rendered assistance, the person-dependent child will become structure-dependent and, after sufficient training, self-supporting.

Cameron (18), special secondary school, lives in a commune where once a week it is his turn to set the table. Because he cannot see the picture, he keeps forgetting the odd knife, fork or spoon. He needs help with this task in order to avoid criticism from the others.

His counsellors have a close look into the things they might be unclear about. Cameron needs a visualisation: for every plate he needs to see that a knife, fork and spoon must be put down. He can do this using a note which he takes with him when going from plate to plate.

In order to have clarity about the seating plan, too, place-mats are introduced with pictures of plate, knife, fork and spoon. Each table-companion has his or her own colour. The picture of the plate has a photo of the person who should be seated in that particular chair. In case of someone's absence, Cameron knows he does not have to take out that particular place-mat and set the table for the absent person.

First, the counsellors show Cameron the place-mats, he is going to start using them the day after. He is supported from a dis-tance, for as long as is necessary. Thus, he can set the table on his own, but remains structure-dependent for a while, because the place-mats are still indispensable. If it is possible for him this procedure will grind down and in the long run he will be able to set the table without looking at the place-mats. He has also been taught this system in the old people's home where he works in catering, enabling him to work more self-reliantly there as well (generalising with regard to another place).

Raising a child with child with autism responding to his different way of thinking in CC, EF and TOM (page 27) can be found in the diagram on page 128.

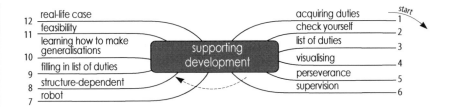

12 real-life case
11 feasibility
10 learning how to make generalisations
9 filling in list of duties
8 structure-dependent
7 robot

acquiring duties 1 — start
check yourself 2
list of duties 3
visualising 4
perseverance 5
supervision 6

16 Supporting development

16.1 Acquiring duties

how to teach the child to acquire duties

- Normally speaking, in bringing up children assigments must be repeated every now and then, but actually training the child how to pick up things is not necessary. This is different in children with autism: you will have to teach the child deliberately how to acquire the What. The following must be taken into account:
- Choose one task at a time (the What) which will be altered. Introduce coherence into your assignment by using 'The Essential 5'. Take your time and pick a moment of calm for discussing this with him. Be prepared for resistance from the child against the change you are proposing, because this is intrinsic to autistic children. However, never enter into a de bate for this only makes him more confused. Present the What as an established fact which is final.
- If this works, try to let the alteration take place on five days in a row, involving all five components of 'The Essential 5'. Experience teaches us that by then the What is reasonably clear to the major part of the children. After that they need at least a week to let things grind down, which is longer than in other children. So do not change too quickly if he does not seem to have made himself completely familiar with it (see also Chapter 19 about the list of duties).
- Once he has been exposed to the alteration for a minimum of five days (using 'the 5' consistently) he has become used to it and does not want to go back to the old situation anymore (going back meaning another change). If possible, pick a period of calm to introduce changes (e.g., not during the holiday season). Do not tell the child about the alteration at hand until you know for certain how and when things are going to take place.
- Do not expect the child to 'think along'. Therefore, do not confer about the course of events. In most cases, this is too heavy a strain on his inability to see the big picture; cause and result are delicate issues. It is more pleasant for him to hear What is going to happen, How, When, Where and with Whom. This gives him clarity.

16.2 Check yourself

If the child does not yet perform the task well (that is, if he does not communicate or act the way you would like him to): do not scold him, but put on your auti-specs and look at yourself. Ask yourself the following.

check yourself: how am I doing things?

- Am I using my auti-communication emphatically enough in order to be clear and predictable with regard to 'The Essential 5'? Check your child-directed communication. Was it understandable to him? (see Chapter 14).
- If he does not perform the What yet, that means that I have not been clear enough (see also Chapter 19, about the questionnaire belonging to the list of duties).

16.3 List of duties

Situations may occur where a number of educators are involved with the child. Or the child must learn how to master a situation which is complex to him. In both cases we use the so-called 'list of duties' (see section 16.9). The advantage of filling in this list is that all five points are being treated, discussing every subsequent action step by step, making the chances of clarity and predictability as big as possible. Thus things are fine-tuned down to the last detail, providing insight for every educator. Using the completed list of duties also allows visualisation of the subsequent tasks by means of a visual aids system.

complex situations or several educators fill in list of duties

16.4 Visualising

Benefit from the child's strong point: learning through images. If you fail to phrase something you wish to say: visualise it. You can do this using visual aids, photographs, drawings, a behaviour contract, gestures, et cetera. Present him with the ready-made visualisation, and tell him what the intention is. Show him, step by step, what is going to happen.
Make an agreement about When will be the last time that this task (the What) will take place in the old way and when the new task will be brought into action. In this manner, the child can make the move from person-dependent to structure-dependent.

visualising chain of subsequent actions

16.5 Perseverance

With the help of visual aids the child learns that the What has subsequent actions which invariably follow the same order. As a result the task will slowly grind down. At a certain point in time, the child will be able to perform part of the task or even the whole task.
By visualising these subsequent actions, you provide the child with the condition to let this grind down if this goes with his intellect, that is. This method enables him to master things,

making him more self-supporting. Do not take away the visual aids too hastily. The child himself will indicate when he is up to that. After removal, keep the support handy, because a relapse after an illness or alteration is quite normal. During the grinding-down period, supervision is usually required.

16.6 Supervision

supervision made to measure

The child will always be needing some form of supervision, even when he grows up. In spite of the acquired survival skills, the autistic disorder will, after all, remain. In treating him keep your distance, but be on stand-by in order to be able to support him. Be careful not to take over duties when supporting him, because this may cause a relapse into person-dependence. Therefore keep your support as minimal as possible and put him back into the What immediately. If necessary, close off what you were doing for him:

Mum has helped you out this once because your shoelaces were full of knots. Next time, you can tie your own shoelaces all by yourself again.

16.7 Robot

Literature sometimes points out the danger of making your child a robot. You will have to make choices over and over again: between leaving the child person-dependent (uncertain to him, tough on the adult) or making him structure-dependent. In structure-dependence he will do things exactly as you have

structure is of the essence

taught him. His behaviour may look like doing tricks, which might be called robot-like. However, all adult persons with autism which I have talked to, are only too happy with the 'tricks' they have learned. This helps them keep their ground in our everyday society.

You can help the child in not becoming too rigid by dealing with spontaneous changes in a relaxed manner. You can do this by preparing him calmly for a sudden change. For this I use a fixed sentence: 'This means change'. Words like these provide footing which is absolutely necessary at such a precarious moment. Give him a few minutes to let the change sink in ('puzzle in'). And tell him if this is a one-time change or a change from now on. In this way you are not creating a robot: you are handing the child a tool which he can use to save himself in unexpected situations. He can tell himself: 'Stay calm. This means change.' That magical little word is a structure he will start relying on so he won't panic (from person-dependent to structure-dependent). The more changes (i.e. exceptions to a folder) he learns, the more flexible he will be.

You may look upon the use of schedules, lists and agreements as a restriction of the child's freedom of choice. But look through the auti-specs and know that a child which demonstrates undesirable behaviour cannot do without them, even when growing up.

Ruth and her dad are waiting for the train which is ten minutes late. This makes Ruth insecure. Once more, Dad clearly puts the contents of the folder 'Travelling by Train' into words: 'Trains run at fixed times, they always do. There is one exception, however, when something breaks down on the train. Which is the case now. When the train is fixed, it will arrive. It is announced that this will take ten minutes.'

These facts are reassuring to Ruth. This train is a late train; the next one will be on time. Father does not really know if the train has broken down, but that does not matter. It is important for Ruth to find peace in the fact that this train is an exception to the rule and that the next train will run as scheduled (see Chapter 4, like a computer).

For a long time, John (10) has not listened to his mother, but now he does exactly what she asks of him. How did Mother manage to do this? She wants him to put away his coat which he usually lets lying around the room. Normally speaking you would say: 'John, put away your coat.' It would be easy for John to do this. But John has autism and he just goes on puzzling, with no reaction at all, he cannot be triggered into action - whatever Mother is saying. Now his mother puts on auti-specs and realises what he needs: clearer communication.

Using 'The Essential 5', Mother deliberately told John the following:

- **What** Be concrete and clear: 'Hang up your coat' instead of: 'Put away your coat'
- **How** Details are very important to him, so Mother tells him: 'By the loop' (on the collar)
- **Where** Normally speaking you would say that a ten-year-old knows that a coat belongs on the hallstand and that it would not be necessary to be explicit about this. But putting on her auti-specs Mother is now able to add: 'On the hallstand in the corridor'. Doing this, she introduces even more coherence.
- **When** Mother wants it to be done right now. But having put on auti-specs she knows that he needs time to process this information first and apart from this, he wants to finish what he is doing. So she says: 'In five minutes' or 'When you have finished the puzzle you are doing right now, you go and hang up your coat by the loop.'

person-dependent

97

- **Who** She can add extra clarity by saying: 'John, in five minutes you will hang up your coat, by the loop, on the hallstand in the corridor.'

By thus formulating your order, using 'The Essential 5', the What becomes more coherent.

16.8 Johns structure-dependence

structure-dependent

You may have noticed that in this example there is no visualisation yet of what John has to do. In this way, John is (and remains) dependent on persons telling him what to do. In this manner, the order comes unexpectedly to John, which may provoke resistance time and again and taking a long time before grinding down. John wants things to be predictable. In the long run, this will become a burden for the persons guiding him and John does not get the chance to develop optimally: he remains person-dependent.

We can further help John by visualising the order of subsequent tasks and presenting them continuously. For example, by hanging up visual aids of the task next to the hallstand, which will catch his eye immediately upon entering. It may be of importance to him that this task is fixed and in the middle of two other tasks.

1. Come home, open door.
2. Hang up coat.
3. Unpack schoolbag.
4. Hang up schoolbag.
5. Lunchbox and notebook to the kitchen.
6. Have a drink and a snack.

'Hanging up coat' now has its own fixed place in Johns daily schedule (the Who), which makes him know when (the When) he should hang up his coat (the What). Also, John knows he should hang up his coat by the loop (the How) and that it must be hung up on Johns own hook on the hallstand (the Where). How has Mother managed to teach him this? During the first week, upon entering the house, Mother points out to John the visual aids on the wall. John remembers the agreement and gets to work: he has become structure-dependent. After a while he no longer needs Mothers help to remember. The cohesion has ground down.

Upon coming home, John hangs up his coat and unpacks his bag. He puts his drink bottle and lunchbox on the kitchen work top. Then he gets a drink and a snack in the living-room.

John has automatized these subsequent actions, but he still needs the visual aids. He may need them badly at moments which are difficult for him (for example after holidays or the transition from summer coat to winter coat). Eventually this procedure will be terminated altogether.

16.9 Filling in a list of duties
Johns parents can keep track of the 'hanging up coat actions' without the support of a list of duties, because just a limited number of subsequent actions is involved. But they do use such a list in order to map out the morning activities. This is done in order to find out what it is that Father does differently from Mother when dealing with John. Because Father is doing things different from Mother, things may be less predictable and clear to John. Clarifying things and using the same approach may lead to Johns quicker recognition and grinding down of the continuous 'subsequent actions video tape'.

For some matters it is just fine that Father does them differently from Mother. For example, Mother always sings a bedtime song and Father does not. John knows this and it is no problem. So it does not need to be changed. When applying structure: do not change anything which is alright and the child can deal with. Just see if the child can deal with matters 'easily' or whether he needs help in subdividing a task into subsequent tasks. Only in case of difficulties parents should check if they deal with matters in the same manner. Behaving difficultly is Johns way of demonstrating that he is bothered by something which is unclear or unpredictable to him.

As parents ask yourself if the implementation (the How) is clearly and predictably connected to the What (the What). When filling in the list of duties, for every item ask yourself: are all five components of the puzzle clear (enough) to the child? The list of duties may also be helpful in gaining insight into the child's development. Every task listed shows whether, for this particular item, the child is person-dependent, structure-dependent or self-supporting.

list of duties is a tool for fine-tuning communication between parents and child

The framework below shows the developments in Johns case:

Johns list of duties   morning   March 3

WHEN	WHAT	HOW	WHO	WHERE
7.00	Getting up	Mum calls, John wakes up and gets out of bed	John and Mum	Bedroom
7.01	Pee	Sitting down	John	Bathroom loo
7.03	Wash	According to schedule with face flannel	John & help	Bathroom wash-basin
7.05	Get dressed	Mum gives John his clothes and tells him what to do with them	John with Mums help	Bedroom on the rug in front of the bed
7.15	Go downstairs	Take along bag	John	Via stairs

- Mum helps him to wake up and get dressed (person-dependent).
- A schedule helps him to wash himself (structure-dependent).
- He can pee and go downstairs by himself (self-supporting/ability to cope for himself).

John can become structure-independent by doing something small for him like setting the alarm. For this purpose, his parents use a small ring binder with plastic punched pockets containing white sheets with one visual aid per page for 'getting dressed actions'. In Johns case, using this for a uninterrupted longer period, the order of the subsequent actions grinds down, enabling him to perform these tasks all by himself, without any help. The next example shows how a problem can be materialized:

Brians parents (third grade) ask for help: 'Brian never stops going his own way and won't do what we ask of him. We have tried everything but cannot reach Brian.'

In order to tackle this, we reduce the big question to a small and concrete component. What is it that Brians parents would like to see changed first and foremost? All other things will have to wait. If things work on this one point, we will start applying the same method to other aspects - taking one step at a time. Brians parents would like him to come to the table when they call him to dinner.

'The Essential 5' can also be used for a problem like this - and all other problems. So Brians parents use 'The Essential 5' and get to work. Putting on auti-specs, they ask themselves if they are clear enough to Brian.

- **What.** Brians parents realise that coming to the dinner table is a separate task to him. The transition between watching TV and coming to the table is too difficult for Brian. It requires quick readjustment, which is a problem. The task itself is clear because regularity already works well with him.
- **How.** When Mother calls Brian to dinner, he should switch off the TV immediately and come to the table. This is unexpected and therefore unpredictable. Unpredictable things confuse and upset him, which causes angry reactions.
- **Where.** Brian is happy with his place at the table.
- **When.** Brians parents notice that there is no fixed dinner time. This means Brian cannot always finish watching his favourite TV programme. This, too, is indistinctive and leads to anger. Brian wants to know exactly when to start having dinner.
- **Who.** It is always Mother who calls Brian to dinner. This makes Brian person-dependent.

Brians parents are aware of the fact that getting to the table is not clear enough to their son. This is what gives rise to conflicts. The parents discuss what would be the best way to tune in to Brians needs. They choose to employ a fixed order from that moment on. Brian will switch the television by himself once his favourite programme is over and will go to the table immediately: dinner has already been served. They discuss this change with Brian and give him a mnemonic by sticking a note next to the TV screen. They agree that the change will be effective as of tomorrow (making things predictable).

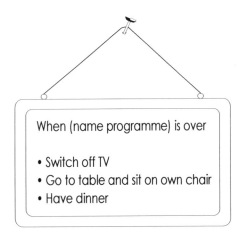

When (name programme) is over

• Switch off TV
• Go to table and sit on own chair
• Have dinner

Brian needs reminders of this new agreement for a number of days. Mother does this before his favourite programme start. This makes her predictable and he can watch his programme without interruption. After some five days the 'switch off TV and sit down at dinner table' issue has ground down well already into his daily schedule. His parents will wait for another week in order to let the change sink in properly. After this, they can start introducing a new change in the same way.

Up till then, Brian used to depend on persons who would call him to dinner. This always came unexpectedly to him because the points in time were never the same. Therefore for Brian there was never any clarity about the order of tasks in this respect. It felt unsafe to him, causing him to offer resistance.

The change makes Brian dependent on the list next to the TV (structure-dependent). After a while Brian will not be needing the list anymore, because to him things have grown into one logical and coherent picture. This gives him a better view and thus a grip on a part of his life. It makes Brian feel very happy.

16.10 Learning how to make generalisations

transfer

When a child has managed to master a task (the What), this does not automatically mean that he will be able to apply that task in a different situation. Making generalisations may cause him problems. He links the What to a fixed place, so he thinks he will be unable to do it somewhere else.

Kirsty eats white bread at school, but refuses to do so at home.

At home, John goes to the toilet for a pee and a poo. When the family is out, however, he often wets and soils his pants.

Situations like these require a transfer. This can be achieved by taking a visualisation (visual aid) of the toilet, the one John uses at home. Whenever John leaves, he will take along this visual aid. It links the What (peeing, doing a poo) and the Where (toilet). There will be more coherence when things take place at a fixed time and coached by a fixed person.

16.11 Feasibility

Whether it is possible for a child with autism to learn how to perform tasks (the What) completely self-supportingly, depends on the following points:

feasible?

- The child's intellectual powers;
- The degree to which the child is bothered by his autism;
- The parents' or the environment's possibilities to understand the child (being able to put on auti-specs is absolutely required in order to guide him properly towards the best possible form of independence);
- Environmental factors such as family situation, housing, a (milder) form of autism in a parent or sibling. All these factors can make the realisation of the above-mentioned action plan more difficult, but certainly not impossible. A longer 'grinding down time', however, must be taken into account. Interruptions by family members will undo 'The Essential 5' constant during the grinding-down process.

Josh is busy getting dressed with the help of an action plan. When his brother enters the room, he regards this as a new task in his action plan. In the next few days, this is still bothering him. After that he is sure again: putting on your trousers comes after putting on socks. His brother does not have anything to do with it.

interruption during grinding down process

16.12 An everyday real-life example

Justin (11), PDD-NOS, fifth grade, has a very associative and absolute way of thinking. One day, his sister Judy (7) does something negative which causes Justin to make an absolute link: 'Judy is a fool'. He cannot see her behaviour as a once-only event. From that moment on, he looks upon everything Judy does as negative. He makes no secret of it, either. No matter what his parents say or do, he won't listen. Apart from this, he decides for himself what it is he is saying and how things must be done. If his parents do not go along with this, he gets angry and aggressive, scaring his parents. In the end the whole household is about Justin. This has a negative effect on all family members.
Until one day his tearful mother comes asking for help. This is the beginning of a change which, all in all, takes a year and a half.

Turning point is the introduction of 'Stop!'. This is of vital importance for the parents to regain their authority. It means that it is up to them and not Justin what he can say and do (see Chapter 18).

'Stop!' - in combination with telling Justin what he can do - is a tool to the parents to make the situation take a turn for the better. Beneath a dominant and resentful Justin there is a little boy who, in order to survive in a world full of indistinctness and unpredictability, has made himself familiar with a strategy: be in control himself. A little boy who cannot say: 'Help me live this life,' but cries out indirectly, through his behaviour.

There is nothing worse for children - any child but certainly one with autism - to be allowed to make their own choices with regard to a great number of things. Children want their parents to give them a distinct framework and rules. This gives them a sense of security. If there are too many things a child has to organise and decide by himself, there is no such sense of security. This is how the child subconsciously develops survival strategies. Justins parents are full aware of this, but they do not know How to change the situation.

Using 'The Essential 5' helps them to gradually regain their authority, instead of complying with Justins demands all the time. Justin has to learn that now his parents say 'no' every now and then and he learns how to be considerate of his parents' and little sister's wishes.

Changes take place in steps:

• Step 1. The seating plan is changed, so that brother and sister are no longer next to or opposite each other, and mother is always seated in between.

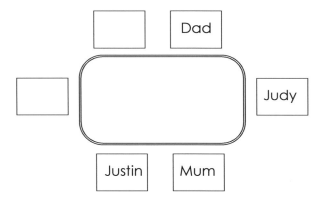

This diminishes the chance of eye and body contact, meaning fewer stimuli for Justin. Also, Mother can keep an eye on Judy which makes it easier to give the same amount of attention to both Judy and Justin.

- Step 2. Justin will have the attic bedroom so that brother and sister are less annoying to each other.
- Step 3. Every negative comment by Justin on Judy is followed by a 'Stop!' from parents. Agreements are made, too, about what he can say or do.
- Step 4: 'Blank time = nuisance time' certainly goes for Justin, with Judy as a daily victim. Fixed tasks are assigned to Justin and it is being examined how his blank time is filled. Justin finds a 'job' at the children's farm, where soon he can be found every day.
- Step 5: Distinct agreements are made in his behaviour contract, for example about who can use the computer when, who can hold the bunny and so on.
- Step 6: Sometimes, Justin stays the night at the home of a relative, in order to unburden his parents and to make it possible to focus their time and attention exclusively on Judy for a while.

After a step by step introduction of these changes, the relationship between brother and sister gets considerably better. Justin is even capable of helping his little sister with the computer.

This example demonstrates how important it is not to let a child with autism determine everything. This is not good for him and not good for the other family members, either. Just like someone in a wheelchair needs to make adaptations to make his home wheelchair accessible, such as installing a lift, this family must be made 'autism accessible'. But apart from the 'lift' there must also be a 'staircase' in order to provide space for comfortable living for everyone.

start
the practice of visualising 1

visual support on the spot
3

visualising

childish?
2

17 Visualising

If a child with autism should function on his own as much as possible, we will have to provide him with remedies, making ourselves redundant and at the same time giving the child the opportunity to really become a self-supporting person.

Life is full of incoherent and unpredictable events for every person with autism who, at any given time, does not know what is going to happen next, resulting in a feeling of insecurity. This is even more true for persons who are both autistic and mentally impaired. Everything just happens to them, although sometimes they are incapable of indicating this. Working with people with autism has taught me that for this group of people - regardless of age - visualising a daily programme is an absolute must.

17.1 The practice of visualising

In this chapter the practical implementation of visualising is given a chance. Children with autism need images, most of the time they cannot expand without visual support. When performing duties or when going from one activity to another, this will help them step by step. They can fall back on it when their minds are one big mess - which usually results in inappropriate behaviour. If we reverse this, we can say that if the child is behaving inappropriately, it means that he wants the situation to be made predictable and clear. Visual support is usually indispensable. In children with lower IQs or children who are severely impeded by their autism you may choose to visualise the consecutive actions by means of pictos, photos or drawings. An appointment notebook may work very well for children who have higher IQs or who are a little older.

In the case when a child displays negative behaviour all day long, and the parents are at their wits' end, what we do first is build a basic foundation. The child, experiencing the world as a whole as unpredictable and unclear, has a continuing sensation of standing on quicksand.

This is what creates the negative behaviour, and for that reason I never tackle the behaviour as such, because it is merely a result of something else. By tackling causes we are building a foundation on which his day can be built - steady as a house. First of all what we do is fill in the morning list of duties, from the moment of getting up until going to school. This list of duties is broken down to the minutest detail, step by step, according to 'The Essential 5' (What, How, Where, When and Who). This makes the morning 100% predictable - if at all possible - for the child. Visual aids are used to support this. The (unpredictable) persons are removed as much as possible.

The security to children living on quicksand of such a 'morning foundation' has an immense impact. It prevents behavioural problems. Apart from this, the influence can be well noticed during the rest of the day. Children are noticeably calmer, negative conduct decreases. The same procedure can be followed for the evening in order to make the foundation stronger there as well. If necessary, it can be introduced for blank time as well (for example after school hours, when school is out early, weekends). It reflects clearly the filling of time (for: blank time = nuisance time). Packing the daily schedule tightly, alternating exacting or strenuous and relaxing activities, is very important. It is easier to realise the filling of blank time when the child already has a morning and evening foundation. A 'book of choices' containing possible activities usually suffices.

Daily schedules are often used in pre-school/ kindergarten and in special education and day-care centres. These daily schedules are omitted gradually as the children grow older, in the assumption that the need for schedules diminishes.

But children with autism will have need for a visualized daily schedule for the rest of their lives. If the child thinks that visual support is unnecessary, he will tell you so of his own accord. This may be because it has ground down properly, so it has become a fixed puzzle, or that he has learned to master things. He is then able to handle it.

He will cast a glimpse at the schedule every now and then, especially when small changes are involved or at moments of insecurity. Therefore it is important to keep this schedule handy, within the child's easy reach, even if he chooses not to use it frequently any more. The really bright ones need no more than a glance at a drawing or explanation. It will not take long before they memorise the task, if only the support is visual, not using words. To these children learning the 'mind map way' is a real godsend.

In order to make a daily schedule you can use already existing visual aids, photos, lists and drawings. The example below is a simple weekly schedule for three tasks: taking a bath, clearing up room and putting clothes into the wash.

Monday	bath		put clothes in the wash
Tuesday		clean up room	
Wednesday	bath		put clothes in the wash
Thursday		clean up room	
Friday	bath		put clothes in the wash
Saturday		clean up room	
Sunday	bath		put clothes in the wash

When handling children with lower IQs or very young children who cannot understand a visual aid, you can use referrers. These are objects which refer to a certain activity. A sponge, for example, refers to taking a bath, a cuddly toy to going to sleep. These referrers are in a compartment cabinet, each compartment containing one referrer. When the task is ready, the 'referring' compartment can be closed off with a door. The child sees this, takes the next referrer and moves on to the next task (see Literature).

It is also quite possible to think up solutions on the spot, by making visible whatever it is you want to say, for example with your body. 'Hand up in the air means stop' is a form of visualising as well. You can use any form of creative expression as long as it fits the child. A few general points should be taken into consideration.

- Be considerate of his stimuli processing problems. Keep things plain and orderly. Use non-ornate forms. Often, one subsequent task per page or card is enough.
- If possible, laminate the cards. This is more hygienic and the cards will look nice longer.
- Use a small ring binder and transparent punched pockets. For the sake of restfulness, use one sheet of white paper for each pocket, with a visual aid or photo only on the front.
- Alternatively, use a mini photo album with pocket pages (one photo or visual aid per pocket).
- Take two small (plastic) trays. Use one tray for cards (tasks) which have yet to be completed. The other tray is for cards with completed tasks. Mark the front of the trays with words like 'To do' and 'Ready'. Or use colours: green is for 'To do' and red means 'Ready'.

The visualising method you choose is the one that fits the child best. For this purpose, you can have your child tested by a qualified person such as a remedial educationalist or a speech therapist. The test, called the ComFor test (Verpoorten, Noens, Van Berkelaer-Onnes, 2004), determines a person's ability to read, understand photos or visual aids and translate them back to his or her own situation. It is the grown-up who makes the visualisation, mostly without the child's knowledge. The visualisation is introduced only when it is finished.

First, make things predictable by showing the cards to the child. You tell him that this will be the last evening he will go to sleep without cards. He will go to sleep with the cards as of tomorrow. Showing him the cards, you let him tell you what they mean. You mention that he can hold the cards for a little while now, but as soon as you two are ready, the cards will be on a shelf or hung up. 'Look, on those nails over there. They will be there every day and you can turn around the card, as soon as the task is ready.'

So, you are being very clear about the What from now on, but you are also instantly predictable about what is going to happen with the cards starting tomorrow. If you fail to tell him, then he will take the cards from the shelf tomorrow and start playing with them, just like he did today. So you tell him distinctly how things will be happening tomorrow evening, when the system will be effective and after which activity that will be (e.g. after Sesame Street). You explain to him how the system works and what you have thought up.

Evan (9), Asperger disorder, takes the card Staircase from the shelf when his favourite television programme is over. He goes upstairs and puts the card on the shelf, turning it around, for the task is done. He cannot see the completed tasks anymore; this would only confuse him.
He sees the card Undress which is next to the other card. He does what the card says he should do. When he is ready, he goes back to the shelf, turns around the card Undress and finds the next card, and so on. There is also a card for Going to the bathroom with a visualisation of the What.
This is how Evan is being steered little by little through a whole shopping list of tasks. In the past, his parents urged him to do things. Evan has become structure-dependent instead of person-dependent. In the end the cards will disappear, but not until they have properly ground down.

17.2 Childish?
If a child finds visualising too childish, it is up to the grown-up to handle that in a creative manner. Because even children like that need visual support. You could, for example, enthuse him by starting from his interests (e.g. the computer: let him make his own list or draw his own order of things). This way he will probably co-operate.
Sometimes children throw away their pieces of work. That is quite OK, because by making it himself he has probably already stored it in his head. This will be demonstrated as a matter of course in the What performance.

Alwayne (4) is in a day care centre during the day. Alwayne never touches hot food, he eats only cold cooked beetroots and meat. His parents are deeply worried because he is not getting nearly enough essential nutrients this way.
When Alwaynes parents put on auti-specs, they discard all regular upbringing methods where food is concerned and focus only on what Alwayne needs because of his autism. They realise that the way in which they are predictable and clear is not yet enough for Alwayne. They think up extra steps to make mealtimes predictable and clear.

1. They use visual aids with each task (the What) Alwayne needs from the moment he comes home from the day care centre until the moment he goes to sleep. Now he knows exactly which activity means what, and what comes next.
2. They let Alwayne join in doing the shopping.
   For encouragement, they let him pick the vegetables the first few times (predictable, giving him a feeling of control).
3. They bought and ate just one type of vegetable every day (predictable).
4. Alwayne can have a look in the kitchen and see what the food looks like. The parent gives a name to what Alwayne is going to have for dinner.
5. On his plate there is a visual aid of what is for dinner (visible support).
6. Alwayne gets one spoonful of potatoes and one spoonful of vegetables. That is predictable, because it is the same amount every day. When he has finished the first two spoonfuls, he can take more, but he has to eat it all. This can be repeated as often as he wants (well-organized amounts, fixed agreements).

This system is so clarifying to Alwayne that, starting from day 4, he eats everything. After a few weeks it is no longer necessary to take him along for shopping. He recognises the vegetable as soon as he sees the visual aid, and that is enough.

It is often difficult for children with autism to finish their meal. Every time the child looks at the plate, he sees bits and pieces again, making it necessary to puzzle. This is why the food you serve him can be an insurmountable amount of information to him. It is better to dish up less food or divide the food into four divisions. This helps him to put things in order. When the food has been mashed, it can be totally impossible for the child to eat. This is because it becomes unpredictable to know what he will taste at which moment and how it will feel in his mouth (for example tough or soft, cold or hot).
If you want your child to empty his plate, guide him very consistently. But make conditions, wearing auti-specs. Which means: well-organized amounts and making clear what he is eating (i.e. not mashed). By dishing up minimal servings you make it possible for him to finish his meal (Minimal really means minimal. In one particular case, I started serving two small pieces of diced bread, then slowly building up the amount. The mere sight of food from a distance made this child retch.) As a reward, he can dish up once more by himself. And has to finish that amount of course.

eating problem

Finishing your plate can also be very helpful in getting a clear picture of the What. The starting time is 'dish up' and the end time is 'when the plate is empty'. Forcing a child to eat his food is not recommended where children with autism are concerned. They really want to do so, but we have to learn how to approach them in a clearer and more predictable manner in order to make the conditions under which they can actually do it.

Sam (14), special secondary education, always forgets his deodorant, which is really necessary at his age. He does do things such as washing and brushing his teeth. We put on our auti-specs: Sam is not 'forgetting' to use deodorant, but it has not yet ground down in his daily programme. You can make this happen by visualising it. This is how he will know where to insert this task into his programme. His mother chooses visual aids. This fits Sam best, because school works with those as well.

Micks (14) mother, special secondary education, has other methods. For Mick, a list works better. Mother cuts short the morning ritual 'film' and inserts a 'slide'. She visualises this by means of a list which she puts next to the mirror. The first days she reminds him, after that all he needs to do is look at the list. Soon, he does not need the list anymore. Putting on deodorant has now ground down well into his morning ritual.

17.3 Visual support on the spot

It often happens that you need to visualise something you want, because the child will not understand otherwise. The order 'don't go too far from home' may be visualised by drawing a line on the street: 'You can go this far from home'. This is illustrated below by an example 'from the recent past'.

show him what he can do

Gerald can ride his bicycle from 'the pound' to 'the pint', which is: from the greengrocer's to the milkman's shop.

At mealtimes, Patrick never stops talking. When everyone is finished, he has eaten no more than a few bites.

- Action 1. The parents tell him what he can do: 'Patrick, carry on eating.' This does not work.
- Action 2. Patricks parents check if they have been clear enough. They find out that Patrick wants to know when he should be eating without chattering as well as when he is allowed to chatter. The end time of the meal is not clear to him. (He cannot chatter now. But to him, after two minutes 'now' is over - so he can start talking again).
- Action 3. The parents visualise their intentions. They clarify the order of things as follows. Patricks plate with hot food is divided into two parts. When Patrick has finished the left hand part, he can tell one story. When the other half is finished, too, he can go on chattering.

Auntie asks: 'What would you like to drink?' When the child does not have the imagination to think what drinks Auntie would have in store, it will be difficult for him to answer this question. You can help the child by saying: 'Come along, Auntie will show you what there is'.

A good answer to the question 'When are we leaving?' is: 'Look at the clock: when the big hand points to twelve, we'll leave.'

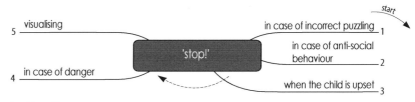

5 visualising

in case of incorrect puzzling 1

start

'stop!'

in case of anti-social behaviour 2

4 in case of danger

when the child is upset 3

18 'Stop!'

Because of his disorder the child often has difficulties obeying. We can be clearer to him in several ways, which will make him understand the way we speak. One of those methods is a frequent use of the word 'Stop!'. We will treat this extensively because it can be an indispensable, helpful and (sometimes even literally) life-saving method in the education of children with autism.

'Stop!' means hands-on

'Stop!' means hands-on and for children with autism this means an order which they will obey, especially if they are used to working with it. 'Stop!' will make the child quit his duties, communication or thoughts. Because it is so clear the child is able to abort his current duty, allowing him space for something else, something which you think is more important for him at that moment.

How do we bring it into action?
- Explain to him that you will be saying 'Stop!' more often in cases when you think it is important for him to stop (preparation/appointment).
- Sometimes it is necessary to say 'Stop!' twice or even three times in succession before it is getting through to him.
  Be friendly but decidedly.
- If required you can make a visualisation out of this.

'Stop!' can be brought into action in a number of situations:

18.1 In case of incorrect puzzling

For example when the child is puzzling incorrectly or loses himself in side-issues. Wrong coherence makes him think incorrectly (incorrect associations), which makes his story increasingly less in keeping with the truth or reality. Or he focuses on long and detailed descriptions rather than on the point of the story, because he cannot hold on to the features of the story.

when do we use 'Stop!'?

18.2 In case of inappropriate behaviour

'Stop!' can also be brought into action in case of inappropriate behaviour.

'Stop!' in case of associative talking

'Stop!' has been brought into action by Ambers mother at an imminent conflict between Amber and her sister about who can use the computer. Still, Amber won't listen. After an incident Mother realises that she has explained 'Stop!' verbally, but not visually. Mother and Amber make an agreement that from now on the word 'Stop!' will be supported by a stop sign.
This agreement will be in the behaviour contract as well.

'Stop' in case of inappropriate behaviour

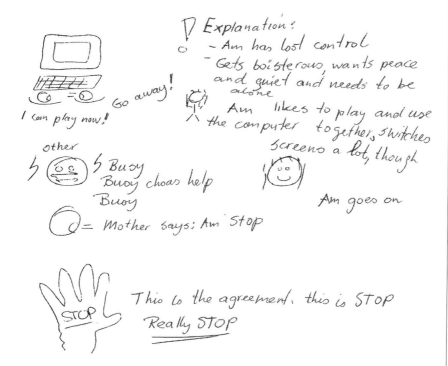

From that moment on 'Stop!' is a household word to Amber. Now she listens to Mother who has thus regained her authority in situations of impending conflicts. She can use a guiding action, teaching her child skills (a rule) for dealing with such a difficult situation, when conflicting interests are involved.

If your child makes inappropriate remarks about somebody, you can stop him. Usually stopping and giving him a different task is the best solution at moments like these, because the other is still there. Some children may want to know the reason why they should do this. At such moments, with the other person still present, it is often impossible to discuss things.

Maud comments out loud: 'Mommy look, that man has a big blue nose!' Mother says: 'Come on, Maud, eat your ice cream'. Maud wants to go on talking about the nose. Again, Mother points out: ' Now eat your ice cream, Maud'. When she starts talking about the man's nose again, Mother says: 'Stop. We will talk about it later when we get home. Now you must finish your ice cream.' Maud still has the 'nose problem', but now that Mother has given it 'a place in time', she can be at peace (and so can Mother....).

18.3 When the child is upset

'Stop' when he is upset

There can be no stopping him when a child is excited and overrun by emotions for which he has no words. It is hardly possible to come in between and to make head or tail of it. Usually the story has to get out, before one word from you can even get in. If he is really upset, you can interrupt him by saying 'Stop!' energetically (sometimes in combination with raising your voice). Immediately after that you give him a task (the What) that calms him down.

'Stop! Let's sit down. Be quiet now. We will go on talking in five minutes.'

It may feel good to the child to be held very tightly for a few moments or to put his head under a pillow in order to be alone for a while. These are all methods to give the brain some time to puzzle and find out what just happened.

18.4 In case of danger

'Stop' in case of danger

In case of danger immediate action is of vital importance. The child needs time to process information (puzzle pieces). The shorter the information, the sooner he can process. And the sooner the child is able to react. Giving the brief order 'Stop!,' we train him to react swiftly.

For example when crossing the street:

18.5 Visualisation

Because words are volatile, you can make 'Stop!' even stronger by saying it and raising your hand and making a stop sign at the same time. If you are consistent in doing so, the child will learn to react to the hand signal only. This may come in handy when in company or from a distance.

Amber (9), Asperger disorder, loves being engaged in conversations but she does not always understand what the others mean. Without any interruption of the conversation, Amber receives information from her parents about the interpretation of certain remarks. (Her teacher uses them, too). This is how Amber learns - without the other children noticing - when something is a joke or a saying and when it is not. She learns how to stop without other people noticing she is getting help. In a classroom setting, this prevents her from being an exception or being bullied.

stop really means stop

Circle around mouth indicates proverb or saying

 Under chin means 'joke' Master is going to use it

Grabbing ear means 'listen'

→ These are gestures which can help Amber, especially in the company of others, because saying 'stop' or explaining all the time brings even more turmoil into her head
This will give her a sense of security.
(puns will be explained at home, if she asks).

7 Who	implementation	start 1
6 When	filling out directionally	2
5 Where	working with a list of duties	
4 How	What	3

19 Working with a list of duties

A list of duties can be a good means for educators to find out, little by little, whether they are clear and predictable enough in certain situations. The list of duties forces them to linger over details which may be important to the child. This results in more mutual fine-tuning for the educators, resulting in more clarity for the child. By filling in the list of duties you are also gaining insight into the degree to which the subsequent actions have been made predictable and clear and at which points fine-tuning is still required.

After filling in the list, adults are often very aware of all the subsequent actions which the child has to perform, each of them again forming separate tasks (the What). This is how they learn to fine-tune their actions – both mutually and towards the child – in order to deal with situations unambiguously. If the tasks on the list are visualised, too, a clear and predictable situation is created for the child. This is how the child can grow from person-dependent to structure-dependent.

working with a list of duties (see p. 120)

For which situations can a list of duties be utilized?
When:
- things are not going well with the child during the day;
- the child is not doing well in the morning or evening particularly;
- there is a lot of stress when the child comes home from school;
- a big eating problem exists;
- he goes on refusing to get dressed;
- going to bed is a regular disaster;
- any 'major' problem exists;
- educators feel the need for mutual fine-tuning.

The list can be regarded as a recital of mutual agreements between all educators: this is what a particular situation will look like to the child from now on (building a foundation). This is why it is very important to have all educators present when filling in the list. Especially because everybody can give his or her own opinions and indicate possibilities, which will lead to an agreement and tuning in.
Take your time, because filling in every single box of the list properly may sometimes require a lot of deliberation between those involved.

Put subsequent actions in the box for the What - one by one. Make the subsequent action as big as possible (you know for sure that the child can do this without help) and as small as necessary. Next, place the What 'into time': put (consecutive) actions in the correct order and indicate the amount of time required for completion. To make things more practical, it has been decided to let the list of duties start with When.

Take into consideration that too much time in between is blank time (which equals nuisance time). So make a tight planning, resulting in a continuous 'film' of tasks. Next, discuss the How and the What. Choose an unambiguous method as much as possible (if for example, to Father cleaning the cooking rings belongs to drying the dishes, but not to Mother, then this is very unclear to the child. Make sure you reach an agreement). Also, be clear and give details about Where and with Who something is going to take place. The control questions below (at the bottom of the list of duties) can be helpful in eventually reaching a workable plan.

-       Isn't the What too big, should it be divided into consecutive tasks? (for example: several pictures - instead of just one - for undressing: sweater off, shirt off, trousers off).
-       Have all the subsequent actions ground down properly into the child's brain? (If for instance, undressing goes well, only one single picture should be used).
-       Are transitions from one to the next task clear?
-       Make sure that there is no blank time.

19.1 Implementation
Once the list has been gone through stepwise, it can be implemented. You talk about when this new method will be introduced. It is almost always necessary to support the child by means of a visualisation. Apart from this, the child needs an unambiguous approach from the adults. Therefore choose a form of visual support which fits the child and link this to the order of subsequent tasks on the list of duties. Prepare the child and tell him that today is the last day that things take place as they do, and that starting tomorrow you will work with, for instance, visual aids.

LIST OF DUTIES for				
Date				
Re				
Filled in by				
When	What	How	Where	Who

filling in list
together

19.2 Completing a list of duties in a goal-oriented manner
A list of duties cannot be filled in properly until you have learnt
to enter into the autistic child's mind. That is very difficult, but
you have to keep trying (and trying...). Realise the following:
details give the child something to hold on to
because he thinks in details. All these have to match before he
can understand something. So look for all the details belonging
to a certain situation and check them using the points below.
To make it easier for the coach, we added a number of
exemplary items to 'The Essential 5'. This does not mean the list
is exhaustive. Find out yourself what could be important to the
child in a particular situation in order to make him understand it.

- Is the What clear to him? Are there any parts of this task which have not properly been filled in or mapped out?
- Check whether the task is not too big. If it is, subdivide it into smaller consecutive tasks.
- If it is a new task: be sure to provide a proper visual support.
- Check to which degree the child masters this task. Is the child person-dependent in this respect? Structure-dependent? Self-reliant?
- Is substituting a person by a visual support important to the child?
- In order to grow from person-dependent to structure-dependent: which visible tools does the child need?
- Does the visual support meet his needs?
- Check whether your child-directed communication is clear enough. When doing this, do not forget to put yourself in his shoes.
- Are your actions predictable? Do you announce your intentions timely? Do you decide beforehand who is going to perform this task and what the other is doing in the meantime?
- Check whether it matters to the child that the other is always the same person.
- Is it important for the child to know what the other person is doing when disappearing from sight?

asking for help concerning the What

The biggest stumbling block for a child with autism is often the How. Let's have a keen eye for a detailed indication of the How. Often it concerns obvious and simple things such as:

-       How must the child do the task?

asking for help concerning the How

-       Does he know How he must perform all the subsequent actions? (For example, during her traineeship, Martha refuses to mop floors. It completely upsets her. After asking questions over and over again it turns out that she does not know where and how to put away the dirty mop once she is finished).

-       Does he know the order of the consecutive actions? Has this order been presented consistently?

-       Does he need a visualisation? How is it made? Where will it be (in a fixed place)?

-       Are all necessities (materials) present which the task requires?

-       Does he know how to use these materials?

-       How should he behave? Is there a rule for this behaviour?

-       How must he say something? Is there a rule and does he have the words for this?

-       Can he ask for help and does he know who and how?

- Has the place where the task must be performed been linked consistently to the task? Is there a clear indication of this and is the place available?
- Is there more clarity if the place is used exclusively for this task?
- Do other coaches use the same name for the place?
- Does the child know the place?
- Is the workplace well-organized and orderly?
  Has the material been well arranged?
- Are there any interfering sensory stimuli? If so, how can these be diminished?
- Is a visualisation of the place necessary?
- Has anyone or anything (been) moved in or near this workplace?

asking for help concerning the Where

- Since when does problem X exist?
- Has a change caused it?
- Does the child still need to get used to this change?
- When should the child perform the task?
- Is there a clear starting time (i.e. the time when the child should begin)?
- Is there a clear end time (i.e. when the child is finished)?
- Does the child know what comes after this task? (Order of tasks is time, too. Making the When predictable means to him: knowing what happened before and what happens next).
- Has the What been placed consistently between the previous and the next task?
- Always show the above in visual support.
- Is there a fixed time for the What? Is that being handled consistently? (For some children: by the second or minute precisely).
- Do all coaches use the same word for the time?
- Is there blank time within the task or in between tasks?
- How can waiting time best be filled?
- The best moment to implement a change is a moment of relative peace and quiet. Not during the Christmas season or close to a birthday.

- Which persons are involved in the performance of this task?
- Who does the What?
- Which other persons are involved?
- What do I do and what does the other do?
- Is the other person consistent in What has to be done?
- If I have to do this task without the important other (parent) for a while, will I see him back and when?

For instance:
I am going downstairs now to answer the phone. When I'm done, I will come back to you.

These are important matters for the child. Optimal distinctness must be given wherever possible. We can never assume that the child knows What the other does and How he behaves, just because we think it is logical. These things are not logical and predictable to him because it is hard for him to understand the other person's inner self and see the big picture. Nothing is logical to children with autism until a rhythm emerges, an allocation of tasks or a fixed order of things. Often these have to be put into writing as well.

Sometimes the child will need to know: who can I ask for help during this task?

asking for help
concerning the
Who

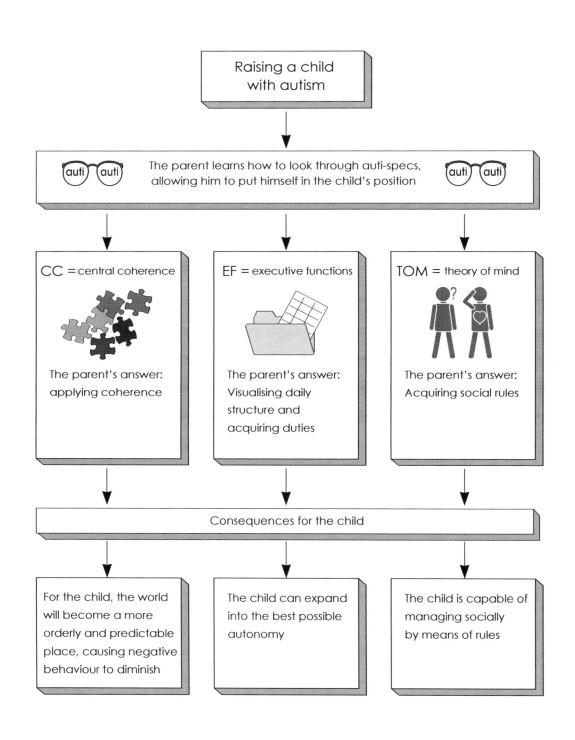

Raising a child
with autism

The parent learns how to look through auti-specs,
allowing him to put himself in the child's position

CC = central coherence

The parent's answer:
applying coherence

EF = executive functions

The parent's answer:
Visualising daily
structure and
acquiring duties

TOM = theory of mind

The parent's answer:
Acquiring social rules

Consequences for the child

For the child, the world
will become a more
orderly and predictable
place, causing negative
behaviour to diminish

The child can expand
into the best possible
autonomy

The child is capable of
managing socially
by means of rules

7 fourth amendment	goal — start 1
6 third amendment	How — 2
Josh goes to bed in a normal manner	implementing visualisation — 3
5 second amendment	first amendment — 4

20 Josh goes to bed in a normal manner

Josh (7) attends a special primary school. He has PPD-NOS and ADHD, which means that, apart from his autistic disorder, he is troubled by hyperactivity. Also, he has trouble concentrating. Josh's behaviour greatly bothers his environment. Josh spits, shouts and swears to everyone. He wrecks everything he can get his hands on. He tears his clothes on a daily basis, kicks, cannot be steered and hardly listens. Josh sleeps on a mattress without a sheet, pillow or blanket. His father has made him a high-barred bed to prevent him from climbing out. There is a padlock on the bed. At night, Josh wears nappies and a pyjama jacket. Over this, he wears a baby sleeping bag the wrong way round, which is closed with a zipper as well as a lock. Over this, he wears a jeans jacket, back-to-front as well and well closed.

If these measures are not taken, he tears apart his pyjamas and nappy and soils his bed. Josh takes Ritalin, ADHD medication. Josh's parents would really like him to sleep in a normal manner: in pyjamas, under a duvet.

Together with the parents, I looked into possibilities for an improvement of this situation, using 'The Essential 5'. We are not paying attention to Josh's difficult behaviour, for we will be tackling causes instead of consequences. Again, the cause in this case is that the world is too unclear and unpredictable to Josh. He is unable to put this into words, which is why he demonstrates it through his behaviour. We ask ourselves the following: how can we make the world more predictable and orderly to Josh?

20.1 Goal

Giving Josh a grip on (part of) his life so there will be more security and peace for him. As a result, his negative behaviour will disappear and sanctions are no longer required. Thus, Josh grows from person-dependent to structure-dependent.

Name of child: Josh   Re: Evening ritual Date: July 13, 2001   L = parent

WHEN	WHAT	HOW	WHO	WHERE
6.00 pm	Dinner			Dinner table
	Play		Josh	Living room
Start until end of programme	Watching TV	Fixed programme Sesame Street	Josh	Living room
Immediately after programme	Switch off TV or close off verbally	Remote control/Saying: Watching TV is over now, now you go and have a poo on the toilet	Josh & L	Living room
	Doing a poo	By himself	Josh	Downstairs toilet
	Go upstairs		Josh & L	Staircase
	Undress	By himself	Josh	Shower
	Show visual aid very briefly	L. picks up ring binder, shows it to Josh, puts a name to 'shower' and puts away binder where Josh can't reach it	L & Josh	Shower
	Take a shower	By himself	Josh	Shower
	Turn off shower	L. says: Josh turns off shower now	Josh	Shower
	Show visual aid	L. says: dry yourself off now	L	Shower
	Dry off	With a towel	L	Shower
	Show visual aid	L. says: Put on shirt now	L	
	Put on shirt		L	
	Show visual aid	L. says: Put on sweater now	L	
	Put on sweater		L	
	Show visual aid	L. says: Lie down, put on nappy	L	
	Put on nappy		L	
	Show visual aid	L. says: Put on briefs now	L	
	Put on briefs		L	
	Show visual aid	L. says: Put on pyjama trousers now	L	
	Put on pyjama trousers		L	
	Show visual aid	L. says: Brush teeth now	L	
	Brush teeth	Things are ready, L. brushes Josh's teeth	L	Same place where he gets dressed
	Show visual aid	L. says: Now we will kiss	L	
	Goodnight kiss	Give each other a goodnight kiss	Josh & L	
	Show visual aid	L. says: Josh goes to bed now	L	
	Bed	Josh lies in bed, L. tucks him in	Josh & L	Bed
	Show visual aid	L. says: Josh will go to sleep	L	
	Go to sleep	L: I will come and get you in the morning and we will have a pee on the toilet	L	Bed
In the morning	Take him out of bed	Good morning Josh! Now we will go and have a pee on the toilet	L (same person who took him to bed)	Out of bed
Right away	Pee	By himself	Josh	Upstairs toilet

20.2 How

how to bring into action

First of all, we will make the procedure which comes before sleeping predictable and clear. We do this by filling in a list of duties together first. Because it is very important to Josh that all subsequent actions are performed in the right order, this is an essential part of the change. This clarifies every subsequent action down to the tiniest detail – to the parents as well.
While filling in this list of duties step by step, the parents realise which details are paramount to Josh. After filling in the list we discuss the fact that Josh requires visual support and which form of support that should be. We choose visual aids, because Josh works with those in school, too. His parents use a small ring binder with punched pockets and put in one visual aid for each consecutive step.

20.3 Implementing visualisation

The visual aids are used to make actions to come predictable and visible to begin with. The situation remains the same; parents put a name to every subsequent action. By means of the ring binder, this is shown to Josh before the moment of action. Subsequent actions link up perfectly as much as possible. The parents restrict conversations to putting a name to the task. Apart from this, a fixed time is planned for cuddling and giving attention.

visual support in Josh's case

This may be dealt with more flexibly at a later time, but tasks must be linked up without interruption during the grinding down process. It would be impossible for him otherwise to learn to master things. Even talking can interrupt a perfect connection. Josh should get the opportunity to let the continuous actions grind down in his brain.
Once the order of daily actions becomes more predictable to Josh, he starts putting a name to the next visual aid in advance. It may look as though he does not need these visual aids anymore. Still, his parents go on using them consistently, step by step, because they form the basis for the amendments to come.

20.4 First amendment

Josh gets a fitted sheet on his bed. It is a thrilling moment: will he tear it up, as always? The first four days Josh throws the sheet out of the bed. The fifth day he leaves it alone. He has got used to it. One day he is very upset (maybe something happened at school?) and tears up the sheet. The next evening there is a new sheet (same type and colour). It has been washed with the same detergent as the first sheet, so extra changes are ruled out. There are no problems.
After a few weeks Josh is used to sleeping on a sheet. This is the first step to sleeping 'normally'.

20.5 Second amendment

It is a calm episode; his parents think that Josh will be able to cope with a new amendment. The padlocks are removed. Father removes the visual aid for padlock from the ring binder and throws this visual aid into the wastepaperbasket, so that Josh can see it. The same happens to the padlock. Visual aid and padlock No. 2 go the same way. Josh takes one last look at them and does not pay attention anymore: gone is gone. The locks have been deleted from his system.

Josh is calm, now he knows what is going to happen. His world is well-organized, changes have become predictable. This is a world he can handle. He does not have to undress and tear up things anymore to show that chaos is driving him crazy.

The parents know what Josh needs. Insight is being provided into everything from now on. The locks belong to the past.

20.6 Third amendment

Ten days later another change is introduced: the jeans jacket goes. This is done in the same manner as the second amendment. Josh accepts this change easily because, again, a visual aid prepares him for the things that are going to happen.

20.7 Fourth amendment

Now the baby sleeping bag is taken off. Instead Josh will be wearing briefs and pyjama trousers. Also, there will be a duvet on his bed. The visual aid for sleeping bag is thrown into the wastepaperbasket, too. New visual aids for briefs and pyjama trousers are added to the ring binder. The visual aid for duvet comes at the end of the binder, at the item Going to sleep. Josh accepts all these changes without any protest. He does not tear apart things anymore. He sleeps well in his bed with sheets and duvet. It is striking that his negative behaviour just about disappears, now that everything has been made clear and predictable to him. What we see now is a relaxed and friendly little boy who can handle three changes at the same time just like that: briefs, pyjama trousers and duvet. Day after the day his parents enjoy this little fellow who sleeps in pyjamas like any other child, in a normal bed with sheets. Sometimes - very rarely - Josh has a bad day and tears up something. His parents ignore the tearing but take another keen look, checking whether they are still being clear and predictable enough. Which means: minding one's p's and q's once more.

To my dad

Autism does not lead to auti-cooperation
automatically. Cooperation going automatically
is not something autistic.
That is why it is no automatism that my father has
helped me, but it was automatically based upon
auti-communication. For without both auti-specs
and auti-communication we did not automatically
have a good relationship.

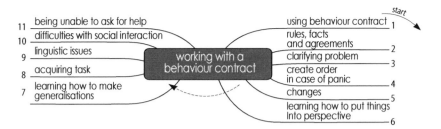

11 being unable to ask for help

10 difficulties with social interaction

9 linguistic issues

8 acquiring task

7 learning how to make generalisations

working with a behaviour contract

using behaviour contract 1

rules, facts and agreements 2

clarifying problem 3

create order in case of panic 4

changes 5

learning how to put things into perspective 6

21 Working with a behaviour contract

A behaviour contract is a large notebook which is a record of everything you discuss with the child (using keywords and drawings). The conclusion of a conversation is an agreement. This contract can be used for children who can make generalisations and apply whatever it is you draw or put onto paper to themselves. Apart from this, they should be capable of form an idea of something which is not there. The better they master these skills, the easier they will learn from this method.

The goal of the behaviour contract is to literally map out all kinds of issues. The child lacks insight into the situation because he cannot see the coherence. Words (often those used when lecturing him) are volatile. By visualising things in the behaviour contract you are creating an image that gives him footing. For example by giving him rules which he can use next time, in a similar situation. This is how he learns - by means of concrete rules - what to do in a situation in which he can never sense things of his own accord.

the behaviour contract makes visible what he must do

Even if it is not clear to you either, as a parent, where the problem is, sit down together and take your time. The child should sit next to you. Take your time to ask him plenty of questions about what is bothering him. Draw it. There is no need for you to have a drawing talent in order to picture whatever it is you two are discussing. That is what this is all about, because an image will 'stick' to his mind and words will not. Here, it is important for you to always take the child's perception as a starting-point.

21.1 Use of behaviour contract

- First, draw the actual representation of the event in the child's terms.
- Always keep in mind how the child sees the situation. Do not oppose this, because you cannot change the order of puzzle pieces inside his head. This is his truth.
- Draw the child's behaviour.
- Put a cross through this undesirable behaviour.
- Then draw the appropriate behaviour.

- Agree on when he should start doing this and how long he must do it (the When).
- Agree on where he should do this and (together) with whom (the Where and Who).
- Set down the new rule/agreement (at the bottom of the page), using a different colour for this purpose.
- Check - together - if he understands everything (see the questions below).
- Find the exceptions and write them down as well (can also be done at a later time).

For example: 'When you go through the door you have to wipe your feet first'. Now you check if he understands this rule. You can ask the following questions:

- Should you wipe your feet at any door or just at the outside door (because your shoes are dirty then)?
- Should you always wipe your shoes when you come home? (Yes. Be consistent so as to make it more orderly to him).

Now you check if he is capable yet of making generalizations to different situations:

- Should I do this at school? When visiting other people? In a restaurant or the library? (Yes.)

If this works well, look for exceptions.

- Should I do it when the weather is fine? When it rains? When I come straight from the car? When walking barefoot? (This last one will be an exception).

21.2 Rules, facts and agreements
When making agreements, the Why is a pitfall when your answer is inspired by insight or emotion. So do not do this: use facts when talking to the child instead of talking from an understanding or emotional point of view (see 8.6). When giving an explanation, do not elaborate on the Why as you would probably do as a rule. Always clarify the Why referring to rules, facts and agreements. That is why the lists of duties (the What) work so well. They say so, meaning it is a fact: 'I have to set the table at 5.30'. The child needs an arithmetic explanation rather than an emotional one or an elaboration on your motives.

'Why must I go to the guest house?' Father: 'To play.' This answer may be concrete but is not the real truth. Which is: 'in order to take some strain off the other family members.' 'Why must I help you?' 'Because I am telling you to.' 'Because we have an agreement.' 'Because children should help their parents.'

They may sound like bromides, but these are desirable 'auti-answers'. Thus you can close off a question for him, which would otherwise involve lengthy discussions with lots of indistinctness. You do the dishes because it is on the list, and not to help out Mummy (for this would involve emotion). When crossing the street, the child stops and gets off his bike because he has acquired a rule for this, not because he has a good perception of the traffic situation. Agree on what he should do, not on what he should not do. Of course, his rigid way of thinking means that when the other person does not stick to the same agreement, he calls him to account or gets angry. But even then it is possible to use 'Stop!', for example by saying: 'Yes, he - or she - still needs to learn that.' (Period, no discussion).

21.3 Clarifying the problem
The behaviour contract can also be used to clarify a problem, for composing one's thoughts. Together with the child, you map out the problem on the basis of drawings.

using the behaviour contract to clarify a problem

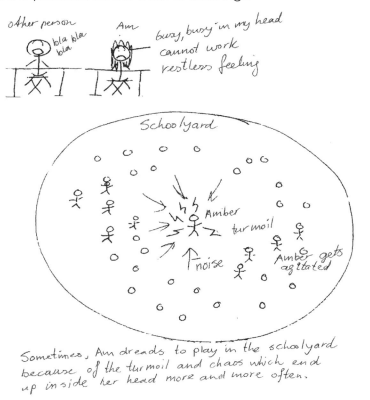

Sometimes, Am dreads to play in the schoolyard because of the turmoil and chaos which end up inside her head more and more often.

Sometimes it is difficult for Amber to concentrate on her work. It turns out this is especially the case after a break. The flurry in her head is caused by the schoolyard chaos. Amber keeps finding it hard to phrase her problem. But when you sit down with her and draw things, the problem emerges. As soon as the teacher is aware of this, he and Amber make agreements about what she is going to do during the break. Together they decide whether Amber stays inside or goes out. This all depends on the space Amber feels inside her head.

using the behaviour contract to visualise an agreement

Amber does not know that when a schoolyard problem arises, she can go to the person on duty. She is not aware of the fact that there is an agreement on this. By describing this agreement, Amber knows what she should be doing next time in a similar situation.

If something happens   go to the person
in charge or teacher!

boys   girls boys

Ouch!

Ricks (15, special secondary education) parents want peace and quiet at dinnertime. There is a fixed rule that everybody stays in his or her seat during dinner. Still, Rick always seems to

a visualised agreement provides grip

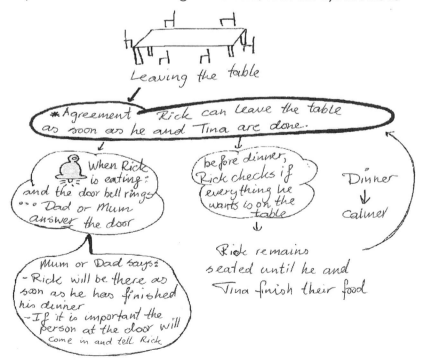

Leaving the table

*Agreement — Rick can leave the table as soon as he and Tina are done.

When Rick is eating and the door bell rings ... Dad or Mum answer the door

before dinner, Rick checks if everything he wants is on the table

Dinner
↓
Calmer

Mum or Dad says:
- Rick will be there as soon as he has finished his dinner
- If it is important the person at the door will come in and tell Rick

Rick remains seated until he and Tina finish their food

have 'forgotten' something which he must fetch from the kitchen. It is impossible to hold him back and he keeps getting up from the table, to his parents' great exasperation. There is a 'doorbell problem', too: every time the doorbell sounds, Rick jumps up and wants to open the front door.

Ricks parents have discussed all this with him several times, without result. When his parents visualise the problem, Rick can see the whole 'dinner puzzle', which sinks in much easier. This is demonstrated by the fact that from that moment on, he stays in his seat at the dinner-table. If necessary, he reminds himself out loud of the agreement.

Rick (15) attends special secondary education and has switched schools. The old school and its neighbourhood did not agree with Rick. Because of his (social) problems with his peers, Rick had acquired a negative attitude with plenty of undesirable behaviour. During his first day at the new school, he behaves just like he was used to doing at his old school. This immediately results in a conflict with a group of hooligans in his class. Ricks demeanour towards girls is too unrestricted as well.

if the child does not perform well, I have not been clear enough

The school calls in my help. With a shock I realize that I have failed to tell him that there are new rules for this new school. How could he know that, if nobody tells him? Sensing a different atmosphere or sensing that it might be better if he would behave differently is an impossibility - because of his disorder. I look through my auti-specs. Rick wants to be part of the group, but does not know how to go about it. So it is me who must make things clear to him.
- Does he want to stay at this school? (If he does not, there is a chance that he will not cooperate, which means I will have to tackle that problem first).
- If he wants to stay at this school, he will have to stick to the rules of this school.
- How should he behave towards his male classmates? Where? When?
- How should he behave towards his female classmates? Where? When?

I am starting the conversation by apologising to Rick: 'I have completely forgotten to tell you that at this school the rules are different.' I am telling him that I have come to discuss those rules with him now. We find a quiet spot, away from the others, and I start creating a win-win situation. Rick would like to stay at this school, but he will have to comply with the rules. While I am talking, I am drawing this for him. He would like to stay at this school and cooperate. He puts his signature on the sheet of paper and puts a date on it. This means we have a real contract. The drawing mentions the What, How and Who, but not yet the When and Where.

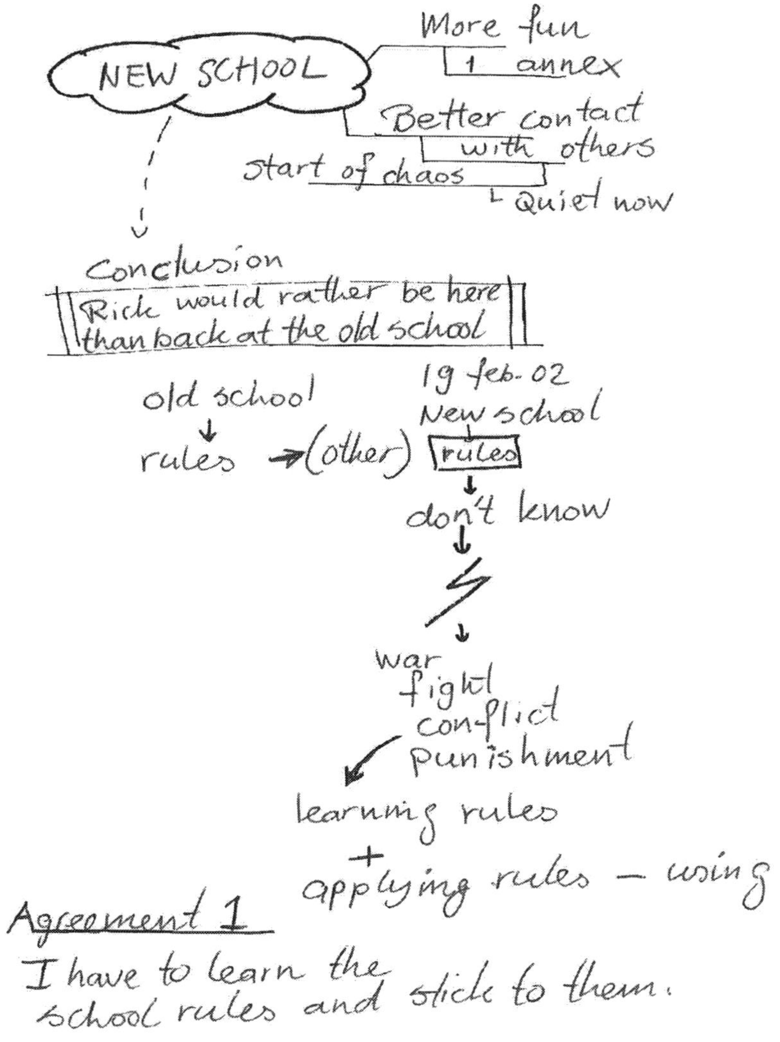

NEW SCHOOL
More fun
1 annex
Better contact
with others
start of chaos
└ Quiet now

Conclusion
Rick would rather be here
than back at the old school

old school   19 feb. 02
                    New school
rules → (other) [rules]
              ↓
          don't know
              ↓

war
fight
conflict
punishment
learning rules
+
applying rules — using

Agreement 1
I have to learn the
school rules and stick to them.

We discuss the When and Where as well and add them to the drawing. When Rick conspicuously states: 'Every day', I assume he knows. But when I go on asking questions about the Where, I find out that we are talking about the Christmas celebration. Rick was assuming that this situation would be so different that he would not have to comply with the rules at that time. So we make an agreement: 'You stick to the rules, also during the Christmas celebration.' OK, Rick really wants to; as long as the How is clear to him.

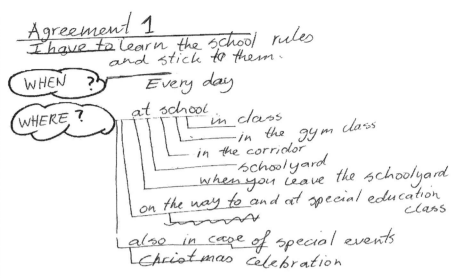

Agreement 1
I have to learn the school rules
and stick to them.

WHEN ? — Every day

WHERE ? — at school
— in class
— in the gym class
— in the corridor
— schoolyard
— when you leave the schoolyard
— on the way to and at special education class
— also in case of special events
— Christmas celebration

I am aware of the fact that, on Ricks first day, there has been a conflict with a group of boys during a break. The teacher has told me what he wants Rick to do: to stay away from these boys. This will be the basis of a rule for Rick. I start by asking him what it is that he does during breaks. Who he talks to.

in order for him to comply with agreements, 'The Essential 5' must be clear for every single agreement

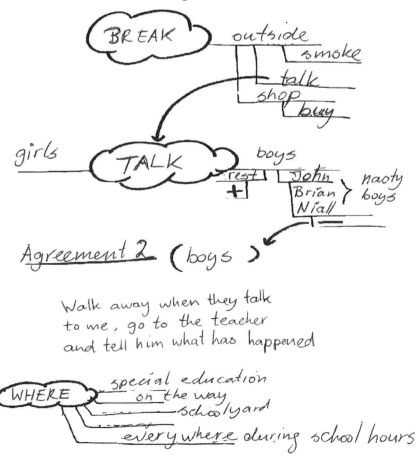

BREAK — outside
— smoke
— talk
— shop
— buy

girls — TALK — boys
rest + — John, Brian, Niall } naoty boys

Agreement 2 (boys)

Walk away when they talk
to me, go to the teacher
and tell him what has happened

WHERE — special education
— on the way
— schoolyard
— everywhere during school hours

First, I start talking about the boys. Rick knows the troublemakers by name. He is unhappy with the conflict as well and would like to know how to prevent conflicts in the future. Agreement 2 will help him with this from now on.

We continue talking about the girls. We have to search a little for the kind of physical contact with girls which is allowed. We agree upon the fact that shaking hands is allowed. I draw this agreement as follows:

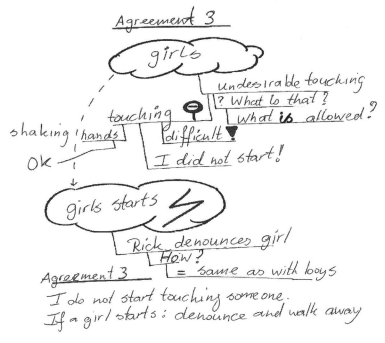

It goes for this agreement as well: once more making clear when things are going this way. 'When I am feeling tense, I am having trouble,' says Rick. 'The rules don't apply then, do they?' 'No, Rick, the rules go for that situation, too.' We put this in writing as well.

check clarity, mind your p's and q's

A week later his teacher asks me: 'What have you done with him? He is an absolute model pupil since he has had that conversation with you.' Yes, also this child with autism would like to comply with the rules, if only he knows How!

if the child loses
track of the big
picture:
use behaviour
contract

21.4 Restoring order in case of panic

'What has happened?' Ambers mother has drawn the facts:
'Your diary is soaked because the school bottle cap had not
been tightened properly.' Mother provides a new rule to Amber
for the prevention of mishaps like these: 'In the morning, make
sure you lock the bottle cap and just pack your bag calmly.'

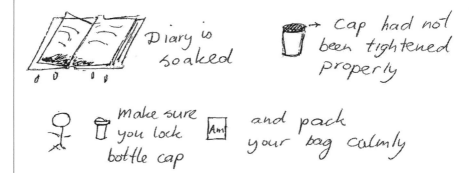

21.5 Changes

You can prepare the child for changes by drawing them.
This will visualise the things he can expect. It makes his world
predictable. Apart from that, drawings can be a great support
for the child's questions or the adult's explanations: to see is to
understand.

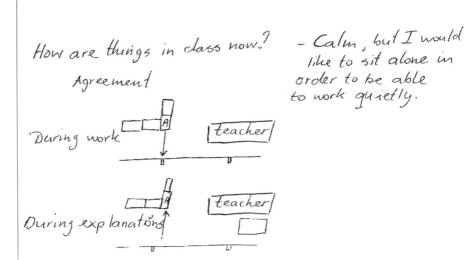

21.6 Learning how to put things into perspective

Minor things can cause a child with autism to get into a real panic. His behaviour may seem exaggerated. But he is merely flooded by powerlessness and panic. It is difficult for him to dismiss these things without help.

A rule can be a great help. For example when the child panics at the mere prospect of something. You can take away his worries by providing concrete solutions.

behaviour contract as a means to put things into perspective

other person

HAHA HAHA HAHA HAHA

One of my sums was wrong
She jeered at me
I don't know
WHY
Is this my problem? No, it is the other person's problem!
So give a shrug

using behaviour contract in order to....

...put things into perspective

...close down worries

Now the agreement is: 'If they laugh at me, it is their problem, not mine, so I just give a shrug and go on.'

Sometimes it is difficult yet for a child to put things into perspective. In this case, give him a 'structure rule: how to act' to hold on to.

Amber

Amber: Mum, what to do when I am on the bus and I feel sick?
Solution: Take along two plastic bags and if necessary start talking car sickness pills.

... learn social skills

Amber does not know how to give an answer when she disagrees. Again, Mother gives her a rule: 'It is OK to say no, if you do not want to do something.'

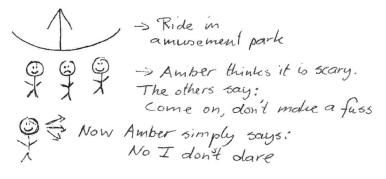

→ Ride in amusement park

→ Amber thinks it is scary. The others say:
come on, don't make a fuss

Now Amber simply says:
No I don't dare

This is all very normal and really OK.
But be honest towards your feelings.

21.7 Learning how to make generalisations

Children with autism often do not know what 'normal' means. The example below shows Mother explaining the difference between laughing about and laughing at (or jeering at) something/someone. She uses one of her own examples to demonstrate that it can happen to other people (including herself) as well (making generalisations). It is all in the game.... (learning how to put things into perspective).

behaviour contract as a means to learn how to make generalisations

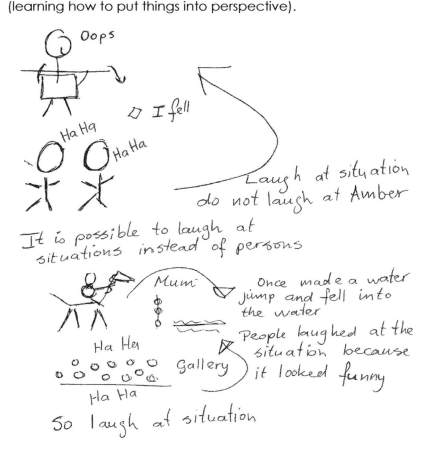

Oops

I fell

Ha Ha   Ha Ha

Laugh at situation
do not laugh at Amber

It is possible to laugh at situations instead of persons

Mum   Once made a water jump and fell into the water

Ha Ha

Gallery

People laughed at the situation because it looked funny

Ha Ha

So laugh at situation

21.8 Acquiring duties

The behaviour contract can also be used for acquiring a task. A drawing can come in handy for simple tasks which the child does not understand. Drawings can also be used to clarify your expectations of the way he communicates or behaves. Sometimes, children with autism cannot get the simplest things done such as hanging up coats, taking turns in sitting in the car front seat, closing the door behind them, not rocking chairs. Sometimes visual aids work. For others, showing them how to do it can be the proper learning method.

When talking to Anne I am making this drawing for 'wiping your feet'. Thus she can follow it step by step.

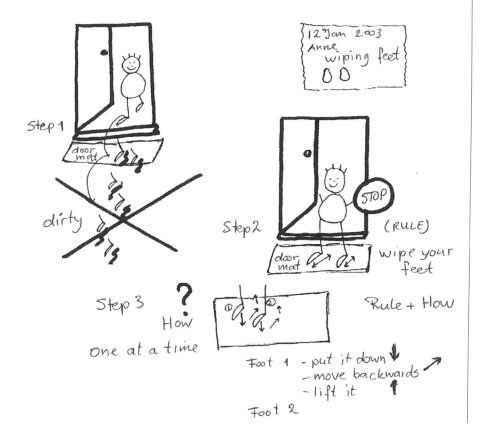

Step 1

door mat

dirty

12ᵗʰ Jan 2003
Anne
    wiping feet
O O

Step 2

door mat

STOP

(RULE)

wipe your feet

Step 3   ?
    How

one at a time

Rule + How

Foot 1 - put it down ↓
      - move backwards ↗
      - lift it ↑

Foot 2

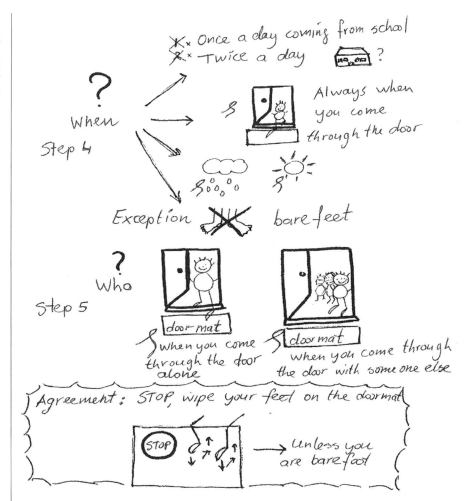

X Once a day coming from school
X Twice a day ?

When

Step 4

Always when you come through the door

Exception — bare-feet

?
Who

Step 5

door mat
When you come through the door alone

door mat
When you come through the door with some one else

Agreement: STOP, wipe your feet on the doormat

STOP → Unless you are barefoot

Every day, Amber has trouble picking her clothes. When she has finally made her choice, she starts being doubtful. After quite a few arguments, Mother decides to make a rule out of this and put it in the behaviour contract. Which, again, proves to be very effective. These 'morning troubles' no longer occur.

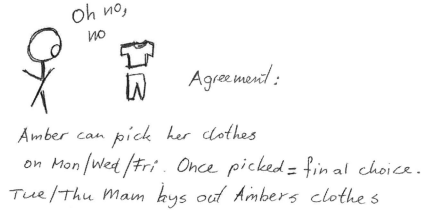

Oh no, no

Agreement:

Amber can pick her clothes on Mon/Wed/Fri. Once picked = final choice. Tue/Thu Mam lays out Ambers clothes

21.9 Usage problems

The cause of frequent swearing, cursing, wrong choice of words and undesirable expressions often lies in the fact that the child does not know How to behave. Or which situation requires which use of words. A child with autism copies street or school lingo and then uses it randomly.

using the behaviour contract when deleting a folder

Again, use the behaviour contract to adjust this. Tell him that you want to hear all the terms of abuse he knows. You write them down, one by one. Do encourage him to mention all the words he can possibly think of. Make sure he is really done: are there no more terms of abuse left in his head? Turn all these words into forbidden words by marking them with a big red cross. This is how you delete his 'terms of abuse' folder (see Chapter 4). Next, create a new folder by writing down together which words are allowed.

After having written down this agreement you may want to challenge the child in order to provoke a reaction. For example, the agreement at the bottom of the paper could be: 'If you are angry, it is OK to say 'Fathead!'. How does he react? Has the new agreement ground down yet? You can remind him briefly again, if necessary.

For Alex, making the terms of abuse disappear is done in an even more concrete manner, because to Alex, gone is really gone. We use an empty, lidded jar for this purpose. Mother explains to him that this is the Gone-Jar, used especially for bad words. All the words that go into the jar are gone as soon as the lid is put back on. He can no longer use these words again. This works perfectly well for Alex. It works so well that when on one occasion Mother accidentally uses the word 'Shit!', Alex goes to her, carrying the open jar so she can put the swearword in there.

21.10 Difficulties in social understanding

There is nothing more difficult for a child with autism than behaving socially. Because of his lack of empathy it is often very difficult for him to have contact with other people. Problems often occur especially between peers, mostly in free situations, like when playing outside.

using the behaviour contract in order to provide rules for social skills on the spot (How)

In human interaction, there are very many unwritten laws and rules. You can help the child by describing these as much as possible, so they become visible and clear.

Special social skills training projects exist for children with autism. The problem here, however, is that children often have trouble making generalisations, i.e. 'translating' into a real-life situation what the training has taught them. An example being: not being able to ask for help.

Girls say 'Stop!' all the time, boys just go on and start kicking, too.

Amber started kicking because they wouldn't stop -> did not go to the teacher - forgotten?

Conclusion:
Sometimes girls dare boys as well, but 'stop' really means 'stop'.
If person in charge does not take action: go to the teacher (also inside the building)!

Amber has been taught to go to the person in charge if a child on a go-kart bumps into her. Now she is having a quarrel with someone else, which is a totally new and different situation for her. She fails to see the connection with the first rule. This is why she is told one more time to go to the person in charge - also in case of a quarrel.

There will be many more occasions where Amber will see this rule re-appear on the paper, the causes being other persons, situations and places over and over again. Until she finds out that, no matter what kind of problem occurs, she must always go to the person in charge (or the teacher).

21.11 Being incapable of asking for help

Lynne finds it difficult to ask for help. The agreement with her is drawn as follows:

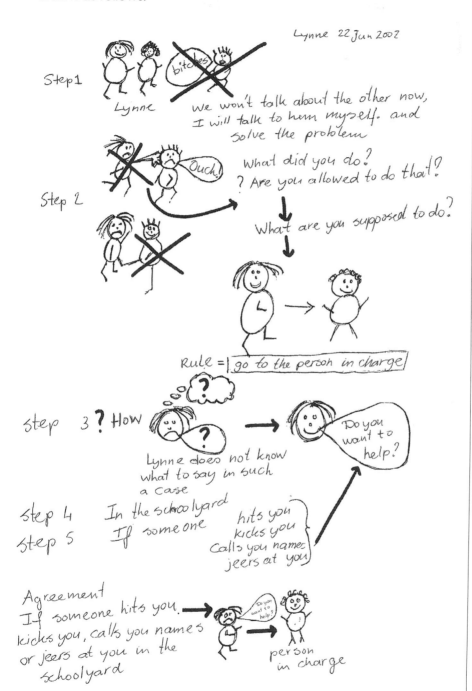

Lynne 22 Jun 2007

Step 1

Lynne

We won't talk about the other now, I will talk to him myself. and solve the problem

Step 2

Ouch!

What did you do? ? Are you allowed to do that!?

What are you supposed to do?

a fixed sentence helps

Rule = | go to the person in charge |

step 3 ? How

Lynne does not know what to say in such a case

Do you want to help?

step 4   In the schoolyard
step 5   If someone   hits you
                          kicks you
                          Calls you names
                          jeers at you

Agreement
If someone hits you.
kicks you, calls you names
or jeers at you in the
schoolyard

"Do you want to help?"

person in charge

147

Tips for working with the behaviour contract
- Use blank paper: lined paper may distract.
- Sit next to the child at the table. Not on the other side, be cause this will lead to frequent - and troublesome - eye-contact. Be considerate of sensory sensitivity, too. So do not sit too close, and touch him only when you are sure it is OK.
- Draw the essence of your discussion.
- Use a few words to support the drawing.
- Use of colours is recommended, as long as you use them consistently (for example always use the same colour for the figure which represents him).
- Use existing symbols, for example: something forbidden gets a big red cross, something which is OK gets a checkmark, danger is an 'electric shock risk' symbol.
- Invent symbols of your own.
- It must be you who does the drawing, because then you are in charge. This enables you to supervise things and keep track of the basic idea.
- If you feel that drawing encounters resistance, just tell him be fore you start that in making things clear for yourself, it is helpful to use paper and pens/pencils. As soon as he finds out that it is to his advantage, too, he will be more cooperative or use this method himself.
- Remember that for the child every change (also the ones you are about to introduce now) is a switch in his way of thinking. Thus, his opposition is quite logical. Be prepared.
- You have deliberately started this change for his own good. Carry on!
- Do not pursue the child's retort. If you do that it will only confuse him more. Close off his reply and stick to your guns.
- The rule must be positively phrased, so must refer to what you do expect him to do or say.
- The things you have worked out together will be put in a folder. Putting all the computations behind one another in the folder will provide a better insight into the major problems and the solutions provided and agreed on.
- The persons most concerned (usually parents or group leaders) have to confer about agreements/rules. These often also involve their own values and standards or family rules. A proper agreement can only be observed if it fits both the child and its environment.
- Put a name and date on every drawing/agreement.
- Part of the discussion is to reach an agreement or set down a rule. This will help the child to deal with a situation in an appropriate manner the next time. At the bottom of the paper the agreement or rule is stated, as a sort of conclusion of the discussion. When describing this always use the same colour and a framework, too, if you wish.

22 Working with a contract

22.1 Contract

Older adolescents with learning problems or those with higher intellectual levels and children with Asperger disorder do not always accept a visualised structure using pictures or lists. We will have to put ourselves in their shoes as well, by putting on our auti-specs and observe the way they think.

Because of their limited 'theory of mind', these children, too, are little inclined to oblige.

They usually only do something when they themselves profit by it. Which is logical, because they look at the arguments from their own needs' point of view and not from the other person's. They often lack motivation to participate in working with a behaviour contract. Still, these children are doubtlessly susceptible to rules and agreements, but they would like to take this a little further. They need more clarity about the value and validity of such an agreement.

Therefore, it is best to reach an agreement with them by using a 'contract', which is signed by both persons involved and bearing the date. They will comply well with such a contract, provided it is starting from an improvement of their own situation (benefit). Cf. Rick at school (page 138).

These sorts of contracts work perfectly for adolescents with higher intellectual powers. It is, however, important to balance them. So check if everything involved has been phrased and written down properly. Never think that something goes without saying, he will surely understand that. Thinking along these lines can cause the contract to go on the rocks.

If the contract proves to be out of balance, or if it does not work, it is necessary to set down the agreements in more detail. Distinct agreements on the failing aspect must be added. He will accept this change if you both put your signatures on the document again and put a date on it.

A child or adolescent with autism has an understanding of how he can best spread his money, and if he spends it on something, if it is a wise thing to do. If not, he will pick it up as he goes along. An autistic adolescent would rather have things in writing: what must he do with his money? This will give him clarity about the wise thing to do.

making
contracts

'Just tell me how to do it, so I can be sure,' Kyle tells his mother. 'You do know I am a different type of person, don't you?'

22.2 Win-win situation

Because he does not always see the connection, a child with autism can think nothing of spending all his money on the first day of the month, not realising that he will have a problem for the rest of the month.

You can arrange things which were not open to discussion earlier by discussing and recording agreements in such a manner that both the child and the other party benefit from them. Thus we are creating a win-win situation. This means that the agreements set down in the contract are to the advantage of both parties. It is the parents who think up this win-win situation. You think of some 'barter trade' you want to bring into action. You do this by mutual arrangement with the child's other educator(s). It should be workable for everyone involved. Yours and his profit should be as close together as possible (e.g. having dinner has nothing to do with going to sleep). But you could say, in the supermarket: 'I know you do not like cauliflower, but that is what we will have for dinner tonight. You can pick tomorrow's dinner.'

William never buys presents for the other family members, but spends all his pocket money on himself. Now he will get a little more pocket money (the child's profit), but with this he must also buy all family members presents (the parents' profit). Actually, this parents' profit is in the child's best interest, too: he must learn to spend money on others, pick and give someone else a present.
Both parties benefit from this rule and are happy with it. William gets more pocket money and is willing to do something in return, something he finds very hard to do: buying a gift.

'You can go to bed a quarter of an hour later,' means a profit for the child. 'Under the condition that you are in bed within half an hour and switch off the light,' means profit for the parents: no more stalling.

If you take these books upstairs, I will make us a drink and a snack in the meantime.

During bargaining, it is you who is in charge. You could set down the agreements in writing, in a contract, so there is little chance of him forgetting them afterwards. To some children, having something in black and white may only be valid if there are signatures and a date on it.

Damian spends no money at all. All he wants to do, is save up for his driving licence. This seems to be his genuine reason for saving. But he has an ulterior motive: if he buys something he comes in contact with other people, which scares him.

His parents want him to learn how to do this. They think up a win-win situation which can be the basis of a contract. They realise that Damian will never spend money if there is not something to win him over. This is why Damian is given more pocket money (profit: more savings). His money is split up into three different slush funds, which should provide him with a better insight into his financial goals. The win-win situation will be as follows: 'We will give you two pounds more pocket money - one pound for saving and one for presents - but we will split the money up into different funds: one savings fund, one for presents and one for pocket money. For every separate fund there will be rules about what to do with it.'

The money is divided up as follows.

Savings
- Pocket money is raised by one pound a week (through automatic bank transfer).
- The money will remain in the account for your driving-lessons.

Money for presents
- This money is meant only for presents for Mum's, Dad's, Erin's and Lois's birthdays and for Mother's and Father's Day. Mum will pay the other presents. What is left over, will stay in the fund for a possibly more expensive gift.
- The price for each present should be between five and six pounds.

Pocket money
- Pocket money will be raised from three to four pounds a week.
- Dad will give you your money every Friday evening after dinner.
- Every month, you must spend all your pocket money.
- If you have spent all your pocket money, you will get a one pound bonus at the end of the month.
- The money will be stored in the pocket money jar in your room. You take one pound with you to school every day.
- The pocket money is yours and yours alone. You can spend it on whatever you want.

Below is a sample contract on the basis of this win-win situation. Because it has been visualised and is represented in a diagram form, it gives Damian a better understanding than the aforesaid sentences. After everyone has approved the contract, it is signed.

Pocket money contract Damian

Starting 1 February 2011

4 pounds Every Friday evening Dad		
2 pounds: savings	1 pound: savings	1 pound: savings
Where	Where	Where
In wallet to buy drink/snack at school	In jar/savings fund for larger purchases / CDs	In jar/savings fund for presents for - Dad - Mum - Erin - Lois - Mother's Day - Father's Day There are already 5 pounds in the 'presents fund'

23 Working with strategy maps (educational environments)

Educationalists often wonder what makes it so difficult for children with autism to understand teaching material. Teachers explain things over and over again and still the child keeps having problems with implementation or rote learning. Experience teaches us that the underlying cause is often failure to see the connection (CC). This is why, also when learning (new) material, 'The Essential 5' can be brought into action. The When is especially very important here.

Alan knows how to add up, but he does not know when. When he gets a worksheet with different signs such as plus, minus and multiplication signs, he does not know which strategy to use. He cannot see the connection between the plus sign and the resulting action.

There is a simple help method: the creation of a map system which explains things to him. Whenever he struggles to remember which method belongs to which sign, he can fall back on this system.

+ = adding up

$$\begin{array}{r} 2 \\ 2+ \\ \hline 4 \end{array}$$ or $2 + 2 = 4$

strategy map is about How things are done, so should be tailor-made

The strategy introduces coherence. When this strategy has ground down in his mind, visualisation, the map, becomes redundant as a matter of course. For a better understanding, a few more examples are given below.

23.1 Solving a problem on your own
These problem solving strategy maps consist of three steps. Each single step teaches the child to react in a more self-supporting manner. This tool can help the child to become more self-reliant in case he is already used to working with a behaviour contract,

or if he is capable of thinking of and writing down the right answers on the basis of questions. This, too, is about the step from person-dependent to structure-dependent and about the introduction of coherence when an event takes place. This tool should be used at school as well as at home for the best results.

Step 1
The child learns how to put the main points of a certain event in order. The adult person discusses this with him. How can you manage this? The following agreements are made:
-           from now on, if there is a problem, he will fill out a copy of problem solution Step 1 (you might want to do that together with him first);
-           what he will do with the paper next;
-           when you and he will talk about this together.

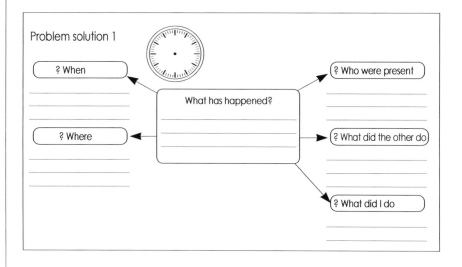

Amber has filled out a copy so many times already that she has made herself familiar with all the questions. She still needs the answers in writing in order to enable her to phrase her problem toward the teacher. Practice makes perfect: while working with this system, Amber learns how to unravel the problem and think of a solution.

Amber puts this drawing (see picture below) on the teacher's desk. They will discuss this at the appointed time.
In the past, Amber did not understand what her problem was and she could not ask for help either. By working with this system Amber gets a better perception of her problem and now

154

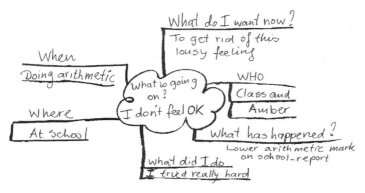

she can ask for help using paper, which is easier for her than by word of mouth. Amber has already made the step to 'What do I want to happen next?'.

Step 2
After describing the problem, the child learns how to think of a solution on his own.

one step further: solving your own problem

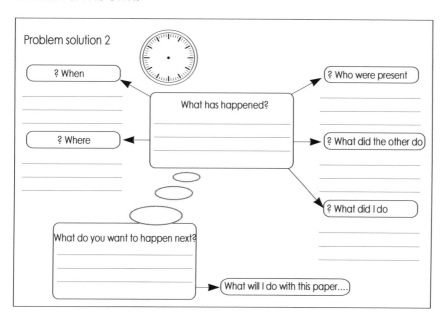

How can you manage this? This step is intended for the child who can think of a solution for his problem all on his own.
The following agreements are made:
- from now on, if there is a problem, he will fill out a copy of problem solution Step 2;
- that he will think of a solution on his own;
- that he will work on the implementation of the solution independently;
- that he can ask for help if he needs it;
- when you and he will have a final discussion together.

the child learns
to solve his
problem on
his own

Step 3

The child learns that when a solution is not feasible, he must look for another solution. This can be too difficult a task for a child with autism and his rather rigid thinking. Make an assessment beforehand: which step of problem solution will fit the child best? It may be best to start as easy as possible (Step 1), which will boost the chances for success. He can always move on the next step later on.

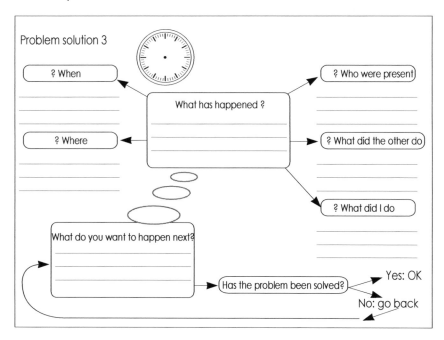

How can you manage this? The following agreements are made:

- from now on, if there is a problem, he will fill out a copy of problem solution Step 3;
- that he will now think of a solution on his own;
- that he will work on the implementation of the solution independently;
- that he will try to think of another solution if the first one does not work;
- that he can ask for help if he needs it;
- when you and he will have a final discussion together.

When a child has used these strategy maps for a longer period down, the questions will grind down. The child will learn how to answer the questions silently. This is how he will reach the essence of his story (the coherence of any problem) and think of a solution, which he can then implement and adjust if necessary. This will happen as a matter of course once the child has had enough experience performing the next step.

Have a keen eye for relapses: after the holidays, in case of illness. It may be necessary to take another close look at the strategy map. Check also if he finds it difficult to ask for help: if necessary make a distinct agreement about the final discussion.

23.2 Working together
When a child is asked to cooperate, this puts a great strain on his organisation talent.
This is already the case in minor things such as share and play together. The more complicated cooperation looks to the child, the smaller the chance that he will bring things to a conclusion properly. This is, of course, because of his limited EF (difficulties planning and organising) and his restricted TOM (ability to put oneself in someone else's shoes, show consideration for someone else('s) feelings). What comes natural to any other child means an almost impossible job for this type of child. The framework below is a reminder for mapping out the general idea of the cooperation (which is again a visualisation). This will help the child to distinguish between essentials and details. It is easier for him to phrase them and make agreements. Putting these agreements on paper will help him stick to them. Which is, again, clear and predictable to him. Of course, this mnemonic can be used in a large number of other situations.

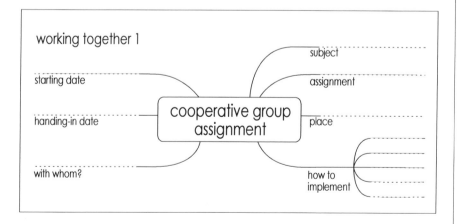

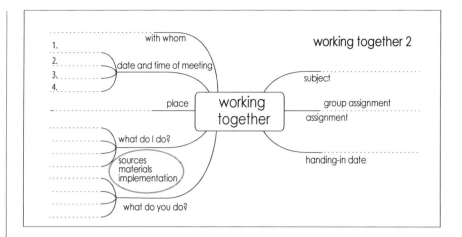

23.3 Multiplication tables

Learning multiplication tables can be a big problem. Not because the child is stupid. No, he is bright enough, but a change of strategy three times in one line confuses him and causes him to lose coherence.

Three different strategies:
Column 1: adding up from 1 through 10
Column 2: always the same number
Column 3: always adding up number from middle
             column

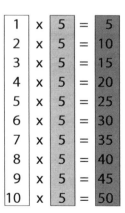

1	x	5	=	5
2	x	5	=	10
3	x	5	=	15
4	x	5	=	20
5	x	5	=	25
6	x	5	=	30
7	x	5	=	35
8	x	5	=	40
9	x	5	=	45
10	x	5	=	50

If, apart from this, 2 + 2 and 2 x 2 yield the same outcome but 3 + 3 and 3 x 3 do not, this means extra confusion. In order to help him we have given a different colour to each of all three strategies. This is a support for knowing which strategy he is working with. This colour and column categorisation will grind down in the long run and will help him in mastering the times tables more rapidly.

This is why the teacher must indicate clearly which operation the children will work with (in this case: multiplication). It is because of their observation problem that children with autism find it difficult to see the big picture. You can help them by first explaining the strategy (using visual aids): how the multiplication table is structured. So that next they go on learning the tables with the help of the strategy maps pictured below.

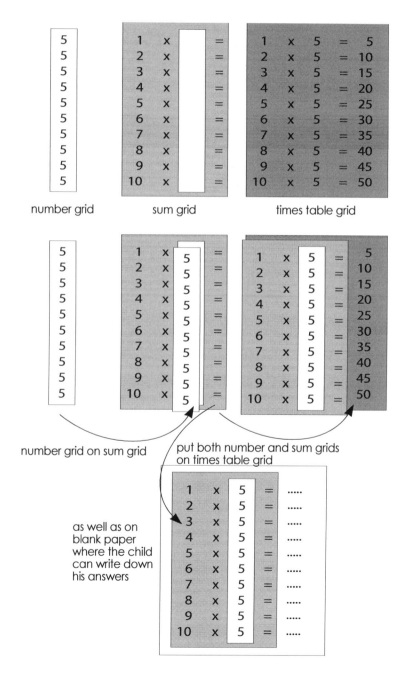

number grid   sum grid   times table grid

strategy map multiplication tables

insight into the three consecutive steps of a multiplication table

number grid on sum grid   put both number and sum grids on times table grid

as well as on blank paper where the child can write down his answers

Make strategy maps for all multiplication tables (see page 159). Every multiplication table has a different colour for each strategy.

The child can put a number grid on the empty column in the sum grid. Both the blue sum grid and the number grid can be put on a times table grid, as well as on a blank sheet of paper so the child can write down his answers. You can print these in colour. The times table grid can also be used to put under the sum grid. Now the child can look for the corresponding number grid. Thus, with the help of colours, children learn to get a good perception of what it is they are actually doing. Use this method to train all three strategies so the child will gain insight into whatever is being asked of him.

- The purpose of the coloured sum grid is to understand that in every times table this information is always the same, and to learn that this column goes from one to ten;
- The coloured number grid is aimed at explaining the choice for one number only: the one that gives its name to the table (if you choose four, it is called the multiplication table of four). And it is there to teach you that, next to the numbers one through ten in the sum grid, there is always a four - in this case.
- The purpose of the coloured times table grid which shows the entire table, is to map out the big picture – which the child often fails to see – and to learn that the answers form a repeated addition of the number on the number grid (for example: 4 + 4 + 4 + 4).

23.4 Making your homework
Roan (Higher General Secondary Education) does not quite understand how to go about his homework. It takes him merely five minutes to finish it, but his marks are going down. His mother makes laminated strategy maps. For each subject, Roan takes the corresponding card and compares it to the entry in his school diary. The card says How the homework assignment must be done. Now that Roan knows How to do it, his work improves greatly.

These strategy maps are just another example and can be 'made-to-measure' for other children, matching their teaching methods.

Strategy map Geography (homework)
- Check if you know all the answers to the questions in your book. If not, look them up or make inquiries.
- Do: read the whole lesson and all your notes.
- Do: what your school diary says.
- Learn: find the essence of every paragraph. Use a marker to mark this in your exercise book. Learn the explanation of the bold-printed text (put your hand on it!). Learn the 'questions' (put your hand on it).

Strategy map Geography (preparing for test)
- In the classroom, write down 'Test' in your school diary for tomorrow and add the date. When doing your homework in the evening for the next day, you will see this test mentioned and you can plan three moments in your diary (mind your other appointments. So plan for days when you have time to do it).
- Plan three times half an hour for learning the test (seven, five and three days before the day of the test). You plan half an hour on the two days prior to the test so your mother can test you. Tell these dates to your mum so she can plan for it, too.

Strategy map Geography (learning test)
- First time: get a big sheet of paper and write down in detail what you should know. Everything! All the corresponding numbers in your exercise book. Don't forget your notebook, copies, atlas and notes!
- First time: read it section by section; answer the questions in the orange-coloured section. If not: look them up.
- Second time: after having read all sections, you put all the essentials of the chapter on paper using keywords.
- Third time: ask someone else to test you.

Finally: an example of a strategy map for making a book review.

The task of 'making a book review' will be too complex for a lot of children. By visualising the task into slices (subsequent tasks) and sticking them into the school diary, per day, at the right date, a proper overall picture is created. You could also make it into a card system: what is finished can be thrown away. You can see that in both cases (Geography and book review) the strategy has been made-to-measure for Roan. There will be different specific requirements for other children.

Strategy map book review

the How of
making a book
review

Day 1 & 2
Pick book in the library.

Day 3 through 9
Every day before going to sleep, read a section
(the total number of pages divided by seven).

Day 9
Write down in your school diary that you will start writing
the review tomorrow.

Day 10
Make the front page. It contains: title, picture, author, your
name and class, starting and completion date.

Day 11
Write the introduction and explain why you have chosen this
particular book. For a good description you could use some
of the following words: style, thrilling, full of humor, imagination,
detective, war, history, difficult to read, compelling.

Day 12

Collect general information and author information. The general information contains the following:

- Where the story takes place.
- In what period the story takes place.
- How much time lapses between beginning and end.
- Do all events occur in a chronological order or are there flashbacks, too? If so, give some examples (mention page numbers).
- What kind of story is it? (e.g. adventure, love story, travel story, war, intercultural, horror, detective).
- What did the author intend with this story? (for example: is it educational, familiarizing readers with history, entertaining readers with a good story, giving readers a better understanding of (a) certain issue(s), give food for thought about (a) certain issue(s). Add this to the author information.
- Use full sentences.
- Information about the author should include: a short biography (about three-quarter of a page), what type of books does the author write mostly, what are their subjects, and mention a few other books by this author.

Day 13

Describe the principal characters. You can construct this as follows:

- Describe the principal characters' looks.
- Describe their characters as well, bearing in mind the following words: serious, libertine, full of humour, lazy, energetic, ready to help, selfish, calm, intelligent, stupid, pensive, malicious, catty, sweet, tender, shy, arrogant, cunning, smart, revengeful.
- Mention the principal character's problem and how this is solved.
- Give a brief description of the minor characters.
- Render the relationships between the characters. How are they related to each other?
- How do these relationships change over time?
- Relate how you have come to know the characters while reading, and what the consequences are.

Day 14
Write a short survey. It should be two or two and a half pages at the maximum. Ask your teacher how long the review should be. If your text is too long, you will have to leave out details.

Day 15
Give your own opinion on this book. This is the final part.
You discuss the following points:
- Was the story thrilling, funny, adventurous? You start by writing: 'I thought this book was....'
- Was there an event that came as a surprise to you?
- Did the book give you food for thought?
- Did you find the structure comprehensible?
- With a view to the language used: what caught your eye?
- Which situation or event was impressive to you?

Day 16
Make a table of contents on the first page. This is a list of all the subjects you have treated; do not forget to include page numbers.

Day 17
Use the spelling check to check your entire text. Print and put in a plastic file. Make sure that:
- no page is crumpled or has any stains;
- the front looks neat, with a big and nice print and maybe a picture;
- the front page layout is complete: is everything there?

23.5 Borrowing from your neighbour
Here is another example concerning a child who lacks insight into the strategy, as a result of which he is unable to make the sum. Understanding the underlying strategy is again a big problem here.

Sometimes there is an unexpected sum in which case Arnold (special primary education) must apply the 'borrowing from your neighbour' strategy. He himself does not know when that will be. Whenever he indicates that he is incapable of making a sum, his teacher explains to him once more the principle of 'borrowing from your neighbour.' He knows this principle but does not know when to apply this strategy (with which sums). Actually, the When of the What (i.e. the task = borrowing from your neighbour) is not clear to him. What he should do has been explained to him five times already, but this is not the case with the When, which is: in minus sums when the top number is lower than the bottom number.

strategy map
sums 'borrowing
from your
neighbour'

This is something the teacher should have told him when explaining it for the first time or rather: should have written it down for him.

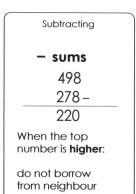

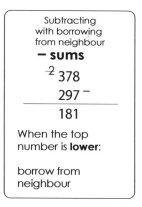

We give Arnold two strategy maps as visual supports for the period of time when he is working on these sums. This allows him to gradually link this strategy to the minus sums. After six months he indicates, of his own accord, that he no longer needs the cards.

Arnold is now able to put into words in which cases the 'borrowing from your neighbour' strategy must be used and when not. Which is: in minus sums when the top number is lower than the bottom number. This is when you use 'borrowing from your neighbour' because otherwise there is not enough left to subtract.

Conclusion

Just imagine: you go to the supermarket one day and find out you have forgotten your glasses. Because you have poor eyesight, you cannot read your shopping-list so you have to do it by heart. Of course you will forget something. Next, you want to buy a jar of strawberry jam but it is sold out. Without you noticing it you buy a jar of apricot jam instead, which your family does not like. You meet someone you know but you walk by without saying hello. There is a young child looking for his mum, but you cannot see that either. Then you come to a cashpoint which is about to close, but you cannot read the sign. When leaving the supermarket, you will probably be very fed up about the inconveniences of forgetting your glasses. It has made you rather peevish, to put it mildly.

How would things have gone by if you had worn your glasses? Well, you could at least have read your shopping-list and bought the groceries you needed. But some other situations would have been unaltered. For example, there still would not have been strawberry jam, but then you would have picked something else you liked. You could have had a talk with that person you knew and you might have helped a child. The cashpoint would have closed anyway, but you would have chosen a different checkout sooner.

In short, you would have understood things better and your reactions would have been more appropriate, if you could have seen more clearly. You would have come out in a brighter and more cheerful state of mind.

Understanding

The glasses in the aforementioned anecdote can be compared with auti-specs, when raising a child with autism. The disorder and its consequences for the child will never change. There is no cure for autism. But by looking through the auti-specs it is possible to see and understand his behaviour sooner and better. This gives you a better view on his reasons and needs. Whatever negative behaviour the child may show, you understand him better, so your reaction can be more positive. Thus we can influence the child's negative behaviour in a positive way
- or even prevent it from happening - by our own appropriate reactions and by presenting clarity and predictability - using 'The Essential 5'. Without glasses you would be probably be inclined

towards anger and annoyment. When observing the child wearing your auti-specs, you will notice the characteristics which make him unique and your heart will melt at his sweetness and sometimes even funniness.

Strain
Still, raising a child with autism puts a heavy strain on both parents and educators. There will always be ups and downs. I have lived through the tensions which bringing up a child with autism may involve, and have experienced this pressure in the families I work with. Also, I have seen the strain this can put on the mutual relationship(s) between educators. Reactions from the environment can be harsh, too.
Showing consideration for this child all the time is a very tough job indeed. When sometimes I fail to do so at home and get angry because I have just totally had it, the others make comments: 'Mum, do you preach this in the families you work with?!' No, of course not! But I am only human. A human being who is very grateful for finding out the difference between looking with and without auti-specs. It is a world of difference. Now I can look back and see where I went wrong. Without blaming myself or him, by the way. These mistakes teach me, for there is bound to be a next time

Growth
This is how we grow together towards a better understanding. And he will grow towards less dependence and more self-support. I am proud of all my children and what they have taught me. This goes for the children I work with, too. Every child has taught me a different lesson. But, above all, by learning how to wear auti-specs, all those children have become my vulnerable little friends, who all had the same question behind the question: teach my parents to be clearer to **me**. All these children and families deserve it so much to be helped by expert professionals .
After every process of assistance, my reward is seeing both a child and family emerge who no longer survive, but truly live their lives.
My wish is that the knowledge of autism and the skills to communicate with these people spreads unchecked. Only then my mission will be completed. Keep your spirits up and know you can do it....!

Thanks

I am a visual thinker, so I am seeing what I am thinking. It was a hell of a job to put into words everything that comes so natural to me at work. I am fully aware of the restraints involved in a translation from everyday practice into words.

That is why I am so grateful for the help of the people who have read along and have improved the readability of this book.

Thank you:

- André, Anni, Anouk, Bertus, Erik, Frans, Gert Jan, Kees, Lorraine, Maarten, Mar, Nienke, Rianne, Tijmen for soooo many things!
- Agnes, Erna, Frieda, Mart and all my PPG colleagues for your editing and good advice
- Astrid, Bettie, Carla, Chris, Ciska, Herma, Marjan, Martineke, Patricia, Ruud and Sandra for reading along
- Amber, Anne, Anne Tirza, Arjan, Bas, Dik, Emil, Mathieu, Michael, Michael, Mieke, Rik, Thijmen, Tijmen, Peter, Quincy, Paul, Rik, Roan and Vera for your personal contributions (isn't it cool to see your name in a real book?!)
- Agnes, Erna, Lilian and Wout (study group VIB-ASS) for the auti-communication chart and the autism coordinate system
- Peter Vermeulen for your valuable hints

Without all your help and support this book would not be what it is now.

Thank you!

Literature

Baron-Cohen, S., Swettenhom, J. (1997).
Theory of mind in autism. Its relationship to executive function and central coherence.

North, V., Buzan, T. (1991).
Get Ahead. Mind map your way to success. Vienna: Hubert Krenn Verlagsgesellschaft GmbH.

Ozonoff, S. (1995).
Executive Linchons in autism: in E. Schopler and G.B. Mesibou (eds.) learning and cognition in autism. New York/London: Plenum Press (p. 199-219).

Schopler, E., Mesibou, G.B., Hal Shigley, R., Bashlord, A.
Helping autistic children through their parents. The Teach-model in E. Schopler and G.B. Mesibou (eds.). The effect of autism on the family. New York: Plenum Press.

Dutch literature

Attwood,T. (2001).
Syndroom van Asperger. Een gids voor hulpverleners en ouders. Lisse: Swets & Zeitlinger.

Clercq de, H. (1999).
Mama is dit een mens of een beest. Over autisme. Antwerpen: Uitgeverij Houtekiet.

Dalen van, J.G.T. (1994).
Autisme van binnenuit bekeken. Engagement, 21 (3) 3 - 8.

Delfos, M. F. (2001).
Een vreemde wereld. Over autisme, het syndroom van Asperger en PDD-NOS.Voor ouders, partners, hulpverleners, en de mens zelf. Amsterdam: SWP.

Degrieck, S. (2001).
Denk en doe. Praktische ideeën voor de eerste stappen in het leerproces bij mensen met autisme en mensen met een verstandelijke handicap. Vlaamse dienst autisme Gent. Berchem: Uitgeverij EPO.

Degrieck, S. (2004).
Werk maken van vrije tijd. Vlaamse dienst autisme Gent. Berchem: Uitgeverij EPO.

Frith, U. (1996).
Sleutel tot het raadsel. Baarn: Bosch & Keuning uitgeversgroep.

Gerland, G. (1998).
Een echt mens. Antwerpen: Uitgeverij Houtekiet en Lisette Keustermans.

Haddon, M. (2003).
Het wonderbaarlijke voorval met de hond in de nacht. Baarn: Uitgeverij de Fontein. Amsterdam: Uitgeverij Contact.

Landelijk netwerk autisme (2003).
Leerlingen met autisme in de klas. Een praktische gids voor leerkrachten en interne begeleiders.

Speel-mee-cd *(2003).*
Als je ziet wat je doet,weet je hoe het moet.
Eindhoven: Sint Marie.

Veen - Mulders van de, L., Serra, M., Hoofdakker van de, B. J. Minderaa, R. B. (2003).
Sociaal onhandig. De opvoeding van kinderen met PDD-NOS en ADHD. Assen: Koninklijke van Gorkum.

Vermeulen, P. (1999).
Dit is de titel. Over autistisch denken. Vlaamse dienst autisme Gent. Berchem: Uitgeverij EPO.

Vermeulen, P. (1999).
Brein bedriegt. Vlaamse dienst autisme Gent. Berchem: Uitgeverij EPO.

Vermeulen, P. (2000).
Gesloten boek. Vlaamse dienst autisme Gent. Berchem: Uitgeverij EPO.

Vermeulen, P. (2001).
...!? Over autisme en communicatie. Vlaamse dienst autisme Gent. Berchem: Uitgeverij EPO.

Vermeulen, P. (2002).
Voor alle duidelijkheid. Leerlingen met autisme in het gewone onderwijs.Vlaamse dienst autisme Gent. Berchem: Uitgeverij EPO.

Appendix 1. Video Home Training

Why this appendix?
Because the VHT method has mapped out, in a framework, the elements which form the basis of natural communication. We have adjusted this framework for the purpose of using it in the communication with a person with autism. For each element, we have made a description of what is different when communicating with someone with autism. By doing this, a (draft) auti-communication framework was created which can be used at the Video Home Trainers image-by-image analysis in case of autistic patients.

VHT
Professional guidance using Video Home Training (Dekker & Biemans, 1994) is a method targeted at an increase of positive contact moments. Watching a video recording together, step-by-step, is a good aid in analysing communication. You can see the parts or elements which form the communication image by image. Thus making the good elements visible you learn to be more aware in applying them, tuning in to the child more. This Video Home Training describes elements of natural communication. First of all, it is important to know how we communicate naturally in order to understand which elements are different when communicating with a person with autism. Video Home Training (Dekker & Biemans, 1994) has summarized the elements of basic communication in the following framework. This book deals with the first part (cluster 1) only because this is the basis of the auti-communication chart.

summary of
natural
communication
in basic
communication
framework

Clusters	Patterns	Elements
1 **Initiative** What the other demonstrates **Receiving**	Being considerate Showing attention by	Turning towards somebody Looking at somebody Friendly intonation 　　　facial expression 　　　poses
	Fine-tuning Confirming reception by	Joining in Nodding yes Mentioning (emotions, opinions, your own and the other person's activities) Saying yes

Receiving initiatives
The first elements which are used in any right communication are: being considerate and tuning in to the other.

Being considerate
Being considerate means that we show each other attention and are oriented towards receiving the other person. When both parties do this, we call it mutual communication. The right way to pay attention to the other:
-        by turning towards him;
-        by looking at him;
-        by being friendly in your speech (intonation, facial expression, body language).

Fine-tuning
This is how you show the other person that you have understood him:
-        you join in;
-        you mention things;
-        you nod 'yes';
-        you say 'yes';
-        you reiterate what he has said in order to check whether you have understood him properly.

The above-mentioned elements are always present in relaxed and natural communication between two persons. Here, the elements are the smallest possible parts. The patterns show the connections between these elements. Finally, the clusters are the major elements which demonstrate the difference in complication, as described earlier.

Appendix 2. Auti-communication chart

For whom?
The patterns and elements of the natural basic communication, cluster 1, have been worked out in the so-called auti-communication chart (page 174), for anyone who is interested in the differences between natural communication and auti-communication and for persons working with Video Home Training.

adjusting natural communication to autism = auti-communication

The chart (page 171) shows how natural communication is composed of elements which in their turn are grouped in a cluster. We have adjusted the basic communication framework for communication with people with autism, taking into consideration their limited mutuality when in contact with others. This framework is intended especially for people who work with Video Home Training (VHT) for example, but can also be a help for anyone who would like to see in a framework which are the main characteristics in his own communication towards a child with autism. Both frameworks (natural communication and auti-communication) clearly show the difference between communicating with a person with or without autism.

It is important to have know-how on and practice with basic communication (without disorder and/or impairment) when working with this framework. Living and working with people with autism always means the same order:
-        looking at them through auti-specs (meaning: having knowledge of the disorder);
-        presenting structure using 'The Essential 5';
-        using fine-tuned communication at any moment.

By using this order you become clear and predictable, both in task and communication. This is 'The Essential 5'. When the video is used, it is being analysed on the basis of all three points of interest. Take your time when dealing with something new, in order to find out how the child does that, and how you can learn to tune in to that particular element. It cannot be done all at once. That is not necessary. It is better to do one thing properly than a lot of things by halves. That does not work for a child with autism, and you will give up easily, too.

Clusters	Patterns	Elements
Initiative and receiving	Being considerate from auti-specs	**Per element** follow receive
		Turning towards him Taking into consideration closeness and sensory sensitivity
		Looking at him Taking into consideration sensory sensitivity

		Friendly pose
		    facial expression
		    intonation (gestures too)
		realising what this means to him

		Agreement Intonation and own state of mind
	Fine-tuning from auti-specs	**Putting task into words** Emphatic, concrete, in detail
		Join in the activity, keeping an appropriate distance
		Be aware in handling him Taking into consideration sensory sensitivity
	taking into consideration intellectual powers	**Confirmation of receipt** Checking subtitles Literally

		Putting the child into words per moment
		Emphatic, concrete, in detail, regarding:
		    behaviour
		    emotions
		    sensory experiences
		    thoughts
		    what to expect/situation

		Putting yourself into words
		Concrete and in detail, using words, gestures, drawings, etc, regarding:
		    behaviour
		    intentions/to be followed
		    emotions
		    thoughts/wishes

		Check spoken language to see if it is has been understood or if it is echolalia

	Necessary supporting tools in being considerate and fine-tuning	**Use** reference items
		    photos
		    visual aids
		    drawings

Fine-tuning: parents

- If there is a (diagnosed) autistic disorder, you follow the parents' needs. Maybe you have to provide information on autism first and how it manifests itself in the case of their child. Parents can recognize behaviour on the basis of images, while you are being their interpreter. Link the behaviour to the cause, which is the disorder (see Chapter 2/3). This is how parents learn to put on their auti-specs. It is also possible to treat their own basic communication on the basis of images, which can then lead to auti-communication.
- If autism is suspected, start working with images and auti-communication immediately.
- When parents have acquired good mutual fine-tuning and natural bringing-up skills, supplying information on the disorder is given preference to. Images can be used in this process as illustrations as well as for the purpose of assessing the basic communication 'forces'.
- When you notice that the parents' energy has run out completely, do not start the communication.
The success of structuring a task will give new energy to the parents first. They can use this as a starting-point for the search for proper communication. At the same time, look for (external) possibilities to extend the parents' strength. Only after this start making images.
- Take into account the hereditary factor for autism.

Fine-tuning: child or adult with autism

- Be aware of the fact that difficult behaviour always stems from undistinctness and unpredictability. So always find out how this predictability can be offered.
- When managing people of autism, be aware that you are using basic communication which corresponds to this person and this situation only. So 'Following with know-how' may well mean that you are not following at all at that particular time.
- The elements of basic communication can be picked up by people with autism. But let them acquire this, step-by-step, element by element. It is all done on the basis of rules and agreements, expecting no insight.
- Presenting structure means safety. By presenting him with structure with the help of 'The Essential 5', person-dependence may grow into structure-dependence. Imprinting and training will gradually cause the structure to grind down in his brain. This is how a person grows into a bigger self-reliance. The possibilities will depend on his intellect and the degree to which his autism bothers him.

Working with this chart

- Always use basic communication yourself when deliberating with parents/educators. Apart from this, you apply activation when giving information or by asking questions in such a manner that parents will find out for themselves.
- If one of the parents has this disorder as well, this parent cannot use the chart. But it can be used to train the parent. His being able to recognize the disorder may very well be his strong point. Thus he may very well know how to 'translate to' and 'follow' the child. Use it.
- Be aware of the fact that every task contains communication. And - the other way round - communication always involves a task. This can be represented as a coordinate system with communication on the horizontal axis and task on the vertical axis. Per moment, both components can be seen on the video. A development or pattern can also be made visible by a series of video fragments.
- You can use this coordinate system to keep scores of what communication looks like at that particular moment. You can see if the persons have a good relationship and are communicating properly and if they are tuning in to tasks correctly. In the VHT, this chart can be used very well for image-by-mage analysis, using the elements that go well to achieve a better communication with the child.

Task/communication axis

You can actually see the How and What in this coordinate system. The horizontal axis represents communication (the How) and the vertical one represents contents (What) or task-capability. Both aspects are visible per video moment and can be used as educational moments.

In the case of autism it is specifically important to measure on the communication axis how fine-tuning to the person with autism goes. This has everything to do with knowledge of the disorder and the ability to look at this person through auti-specs and thus tuning in to him. With regard to the task axis it is important to measure whether a person's task-capability is sufficient and if he tunes in to the child with autism. This, too, requires knowledge of the disorder, resulting in proper fine-tuning. Both axes should be balanced.

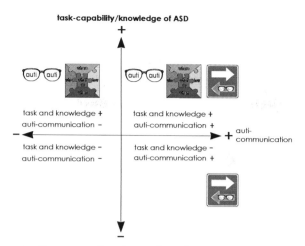

Keeping scores in the coordinate system is done as follows.

-   In the left hand bottom corner: both axes have a minus. This person does not yet have a good basic communication. He has no knowledge yet of the autistic disorder and as a result cannot tune in to the child with autism with a view to tasks and communication.

-   In the left hand top corner: the task/knowledge axis has a plus, and the communication axis has a minus. This person is capable of putting himself in the autistic child's shoes and can fine-tune tasks, but the communication with the child is not good yet.

-   In the right hand bottom corner: the task/communication axis has a minus and the communication axis has a plus. This means that this person has good basic communication, but is not yet geared to autism: he does not have the knowledge yet.
    Because of the lack of knowledge of autism the tasks have not been fine-tuned either.

-   In the right hand top corner: both axes have a plus. This person knows how to put himself in the child's mind, can fine-tune tasks and knows how to discuss these with the child properly. So, a (VHT) training always involves learning how to look through auti-specs (knowledge of autism) as well as learning how to work with basic communication and auti-communication. Thus, it becomes possible to learn how to deal with people with autism so they feel understood.
    The video analysis of auti-communication is a specialist form of Video Home Training. People working with VHT must have additional training.

Both the auti-communication chart and the coordinate system for autism have been developed by the study group VIB-ASS (May 2004).

Appendix 3. The practice of visualisation

Alexanders Books
week book

Alexander (9), general education, has made drawings of all the tasks he must do in the morning before going to school and put them in a nice little book. He has done this of his own accord. Alexander uses his book daily and is very proud of it. Still, at the beginning of the week, mornings go by less smoothly than at the end. Alexander gets confused because the weekend has a different rhythm. A weekend book is made for Alexander as well (see page 184). Now he can use a book as a visual support every day. The mornings have gone smoothly ever since. It is much easier for Alexander to get to his tasks in the weekend as well. Everything has been put 'into time' (WHEN).

Waking up

Wash

Put on clean socks and underwear

Get dressed

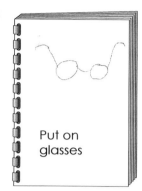

Put on glasses

Drink & eat bread

Brush teeth

Comb hair

Put on coat and pack schoolbag

Go to the bus

 *weekend book*

Sleep late

Wash

Put on clean socks and underwear

Get dressed

Comb hair

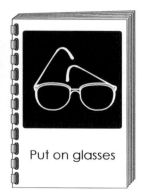

Put on glasses

Drink & eat

Brush teeth

Chores

Be lazy

Potter

Play games

Computer
time

Watch TV

Fine-tuning rules

Alex behaves pigheaded whenever there is a baby-sitter. Mother thinks that Alex is troubled by the changes involved in another person. To help with this she makes a list of agreements for the baby-sitter. Alex reads this list beforehand. He is now prepared how things will go once the baby-sitter is there. The list makes it clear to both parties What Alex is going to do, How, Where, When and with Who.

182

Reminder for the road

It may be just a few yards, but Benjamin never seems to reach his destination. He is distracted by everything he sees on his way and forgets his assignment. Vera, his group leader, has thought of the following to teach Benjamin structure-dependence. She puts three visual aids on Benjamins sleeve, using Velcro. From a box, Vera picks exactly those visual aids Benjamin needs and sticks them to his sleeve. On the way the visual aids keep catching Benjamins eye, reminding him of his assignment.

Newspaper

Go shopping

Coca-Cola

Getting rid of anger

Marks guardian (16, special secondary education) has cancelled their appointment because he is ill. Three days later no new date has been set yet. Marks body language demonstrates that he is unhappy about something. He throws himself on the ground and walks away crossly. He has no words to express why he is angry. Still angry, Mark is taken to his day-care centre. When he arrives there he is still grumbling. Elsa, one of the coaches, think s she knows what is going on. The folder 'Appointment with Richard (guardian)' is still open. She cannot close it for Mark. What she can do, is put the solution 'into time'. Here is how she does that: she agrees with Mark that, as soon as the guardian comes home from work, they will call him. In order to hold on to that appointment during the day, she visualises it by drawing it on Marks arm. Now Mark finds clarity. He knows now what is going to happen. His angry fit is over within a minute.

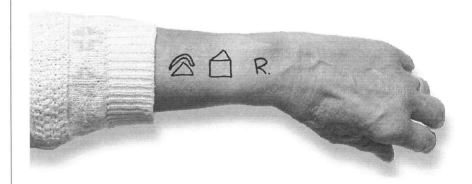

17406521R00100

Printed in Great Britain
by Amazon